Photographs by

Ernest C. Jaco
California State College
    at Hayward

Original line drawings of
fireflies by

Esther M. Osnas
San Francisco, California

enrichment ideas

literature for children

Pose Lamb
Consulting Editor
Purdue University

Storytelling and Creative Drama—*Dewey W. Chambers, University of the Pacific, Stockton, California*

Illustrations in Children's Books—*Patricia Cianciolo, Michigan State University*

Enrichment Ideas—*Ruth Kearney Carlson, California State College at Hayward*

History and Trends—*Margaret C. Gillespie, Marquette University*

Poetry in the Elementary School—*Virginia Witucke, Purdue University*

Its Discipline and Content—*Bernice Cullinan, New York University*

Children's Literature in the Curriculum—*Mary Montebello, State University of New York at Buffalo*

enrichment
ideas
sparkling fireflies

RUTH KEARNEY CARLSON
California State College,
Hayward

Pose Lamb
Consulting Editor
Purdue University

WM. C. BROWN COMPANY PUBLISHERS
Dubuque, Iowa

Printed in the United States of America

Dedicated to students of my classes at California State College at Hayward who have generously shared their creative thoughts and enrichment ideas with others.

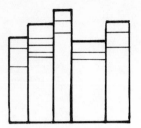

contents

foreword

This series of books came to be because of the editor's conviction that most textbooks about literature for children had not been written for elementary teachers, regardless of the anticipated audience suggested by the titles. The words, *Literature for Children*, preceding each individual title indicate not only the respect for the field held by the authors and the editor but our evaluation of the importance of this type of literature, worthy of consideration along with other categories or classifications of English literature. However, it is *what happens* through books, and the *uses* of literature which are of concern to the authors of this series, as well as the provision of an historical perspective and some knowledge of the writer's and the illustrator's crafts. Our work, then, is directed primarily to the elementary classroom teacher who wants to design and implement an effective program of literature for children.

Because entire books have been devoted to specific topics, for example, the history of literature for children, it is hoped that such topics are covered in greater depth than usual. They are not merely books *about* children's literature; the focus in this series is on helping teachers see what literature for children has been, the direction or directions pointed by scholars in the field, and some ways in which a teacher can share with children the excitement and joy of reading. The authors have tried to share with teachers and prospective teachers their enthusiasm for children's literature, today's and yesterday's; for an unenthusiastic teacher, though well-informed, will not communicate enthusiasm to his pupils.

The author of each book was selected, first because he has demonstrated this enthusiasm in his teaching and writing, and secondly because of his competence in the field of children's literature in general. It is hoped that the thoroughness and depth with which each topic has been explored and the expertise which each author has brought to a topic in which he has a particular interest will serve as sufficient justifications for such a venture.

Children's literature courses are among the most popular courses in the professional sequence at many colleges and universities. It is rewarding and exciting to re-enter the world of literature for children, to experience again the joy of encountering a new author or of renewing acquaintance with a favorite author or a character created by an author.

The editor and the authors of this series have tried to capture the magic that is literature for children and to provide some help for teachers who want to share that *magic with children.*

Emphasis on the uses of literature for children, techniques for applying, exhibiting, sharing what one knows about it, has been a characteristic of the entire series. Certainly, this has been one of the most important objectives of the editor and the authors.

Nevertheless, those responsible for planning this series identified the need for an entire book devoted to teaching ideas, and instructional strategies, with some facet of literature for children as their core. The reader is undoubtedly aware of the work of Ruth Kearney Carlson, and it is fortunate for the publisher, the editor, and certainly for the reader that she directed her tremendous creative talents toward this project.

The reader will find more ideas in this books, more suggestions for dramatization, art projects, language games, and suggestions for using literature to enrich each facet of the curriculum than he can utilize in several years of teaching. Furthermore, an interesting thing about a project of this type is that each idea the author presents will almost certainly stimulate several more! This is surely what the author intended.

In *Literature for Children: Enrichment Ideas,* the reader will find a provocative and knowledgeable discussion of the following:

—what elements of the classroom environment can be used to give support to and enrich the literature program?

—what activities can the teacher plan and guide which will enhance the literature program in the elementary schools?

—literature can be used to enrich various curricular areas—what materials are best for this? What books can be used to make the language program more meaningful? Has literature anything to offer in terms of enriching and supporting the social studies program? What about science?

There's another function of literature, sometimes called bibliotherapy, with which the author deals with perception and sensitivity.
Each of us is occasionally lonely, and fearful. Writers of children's books
have had these experiences, and some have written about their experiences in ways which can lift the human spirit.

Pose Lamb, Editor

preface

A famous Japanese poet, Issa, expresses beauty in his *haiku* verse with its glimpse of a giant firefly tracing its path this way and that way as it flits about. Another image of fireflies offers a sense of contemplation and revelation. One quietly sits by the sea, or by a pond, and revels in the wonders of the universe. Nothing is insignificant—the rocking gull folding its wing in silent sleep—rose-red peonies scattering their petals in the wind, or a delicate fragile cobweb dropping diamond dewdrops after a spring shower. Children should experience literature which has inherent beauty in both words and thought.

Boys and girls can be exposed to much of the finest literature of our culture, but if their imaginations are not kindled by some spark which relates them to the spoken word or the printed page, their literary experiences may become a series of unrelated sound utterances, or a procession of black, blurred sticks walking across a snow-white page.

It is hoped that some pages in *Enrichment Ideas* capture a bit of the excitement which lies in the large number of books available to the modern child. As a pupil opens up the pages of a book, perhaps he can reiterate the words of Hopkins who said, "What I do is me, for that I came."

R. K. C.

chapter 1

from birds to stones,
the miracle of language

The miracle of human language commences with man's first utterance which was communicated meaningfully to another person. Long ago, in ancient Egypt, a weird-looking god, Throth, was worshipped reverently. His head was the sacred Ibis, and his hands carried a reed brush and an ink palette. It was Throth who supposedly bequeathed a system of sacred writing, or hieroglyphics.

Early Writing

The significance of hieroglyphic writing was not grasped until many centuries later. In the summer of 1799, a soldier in Napoleon's engineering corps discovered an interesting black stone inscribed with odd characters. This later became known as the Rosetta stone. It was a significant discovery, for carvings depicted three kinds of writing: Egyptian hieroglyphics, a demotic style of ordinary writing, and Greek inscriptions. Jean François Champollion made a career of seeking clues concerning the stone's message. He fortunately remembered seeing, on an island in the Nile River, an obelisk which depicted Greek inscriptions at the base and hieroglyphs above, with the names *Ptolemy* and *Cleopatra* in Greek. He and other scholars used clues from this obelisk, the Rosetta stone, and carved inscriptions on other monuments to unlock the written language of the ancient Egyptians. The mighty eagle was the hieroglyph for A. This bird was so highly admired that it later became the symbol for the *soul*.

This and many other fascinating stories about our alphabet and language appear in *The 26 Letters,* written and illustrated by a foremost American calligrapher, Oscar Ogg, (Thomas Y. Crowell Company).

1

The volume depicts wily Phoenicians trafficking in ivory, tin, spices, perfumes, and the slave trade. It was in Byblos, the Phoenician capitol, that a profitable papyrus trade was conducted, and many parts of the alphabet were borrowed from the Assyrians and Babylonians as well as from the Egyptians.

Around 200 B.C., when papyrus became scarce, a young scribe in Pergamus, Asia Minor, invented parchment. He split the skin of a kid, goat, or sheep, bleached it, and then pounded and rubbed it until he had a smooth surface for writing. Parchment was highly valued until cheaper paper became popular.

Early Printing

Many, many years elapsed from this time until the period when Johann Gutenberg radically changed the demand for paper through the perfection of a movable press. The famous Gutenberg Bible was printed in 1456. Long before this time, some Chinese scholars published books by using characters carved from wooden blocks, and in 1337, they printed a book by using movable blocks. The distinction of inventing printing, however, was given to Gutenberg since the Gutenberg Bible had been considered to be the first published book which used movable metal type cast in molds. Some details about this inventor's struggles to improve printing processes appear in *The 26 Letters*.

Gutenberg is credited with many discoveries related to printing, but William Caxton is known as "the father of English printing." He was born in England in 1422. His principal business was that of a mercer or cloth merchant, but later in life, he became interested in publishing documents and books. He traveled to Cologne in 1471-1472 to learn the printing trade. Here, he and a French scribe, Colard Mansion, designed and cut an English type which was Dutch Gothic in style. Then Caxton translated a collection of French romances based on Trojan history and printed them in English in 1475 or 1476. A year or so later, he set up his press in Westminster, a London suburb. Here he worked, principally at printing, until his death in 1491. He printed Chaucer's *Canterbury Tales* and Malory's *Morte d'Arthur*.

An interesting historical novel which is mostly about Caxton and his battle with scriveners is *Caxton's Challenge* which was written and illustrated by Cynthia Harnett (The World Publishing Co.). This is a fictionalized account which focuses upon the antagonism between Bendy and his older brother, Matthew, who resents Caxton and printing presses. He fears that his profitable scrivener shop will be bankrupted by speedier duplication processes. Tom Twist, a wily peddler, succeeds in intercepting shipments of Unicorn paper and clandestinely selling them to Matthew. Bendy possesses portions of some rare handwritten tales about King Arthur, by Sir Thomas Malory. Much of the Harnett novel consists of the quest for missing portions of this manuscript.

Chaucer and His World

Caxton popularized *The Canterbury Tales* by making them more accessible to the English reading public. Some of Chaucer is too difficult for youngsters to understand, but Anne Malcolmson selected and edited some of *The Canterbury Tales* for her volume, *A Taste of Chaucer,* with illustrations by Enrico Arno (Harcourt, Brace & World). This book is for older pupils, and the selections include the prologue and nine of the stories, among them "Chanticleer and the Fox," "The Wily Alchemist," "Patient Griselda," "Phoebus and the Crow," and others. An introduction gives some biographical details about Chaucer and his writings. *Chanticleer and the Fox,* edited and illustrated by Barbara Cooney, is a popular Chaucer tale which can be understood by primary age boys and girls. This book was published by Thomas Y. Crowell in 1958 and won the Caldecott book award for the most distinguished picture book of the year.

Other Books about Chaucer

In recent years, several books about Chaucer have been written for children. Marie Neurath and John Ellis wrote *They Lived Like This in Chaucer's England* (Franklin Watts). The illustrations depict scribes at writing desks sharpening their quills. Initial letters for chapters incorporate pictures. An S, for example, has two scenes . . . the top part of the letter shows God extending his hands through the clouds, and the lower part shows Jonah being swallowed by a whale. Scenes of lords, and of villagers tending sheep are depicted, as well as pictures of wooden ships, bows, arrows, spears, pickaxes, and an English longbow.

Another book for older pupils is *Chaucer and His World* by Ian Serraillier (Henry Z. Walck). This volume brings to life Chaucer's England. It tells that Chaucer was born at some time between 1340 and 1345, that he was tutored, and that he wrote a volume of poems titled *The Book of the Duchess* in 1369 when he was a page in the duchess' household.

In Chaucer's time, London was a walled town with narrow overhanging upper-floor structures located above the walls. Traffic flowed in and out of the walled city during the day, but the gates were closed at night so as to protect citizens from invaders and bandits. Chaucer became Comptroller of the Customs for the wool trade in 1376 and superintended the collection of duties from vessels exporting English wool. His appointment entitled him to quarters over Algate, an eastern wall of London. Here he wrote several long narrative poems, including "Troilus and Criseyde."

Life in London then was considerably different from modern times. Hawkers sold wares on the streets. Many persons kept sheep so as to have milk, wool, and meat. All ranks of society spun wool. At that time, utensils for cooking and eating were sparse. Spoons were cast of tin. Cooks used huge bronze caldrons for cooking, cleavers and fleshing hooks for meat, and long shovels for removing loaves of bread from the oven.

Other books giving background on English life and literature are ones such as those by Ivor Brown titled *Shakespeare and His World, Doctor Johnson and His World,* and *Jane Austin and Her World* (Henry Z. Walck). These volumes were written for older adolescent readers, but advanced sixth and seventh grade pupils might enjoy their factual details.

Framework of The Canterbury Tales

In Chaucer's time, authors frequently set a group of stories in a larger framework. Chaucer chose this format for his volume, *The Canterbury Tales,* because he wanted to include a variety of narratives written in different styles and presenting variant points of view. He created a group of pilgrims who had more wanderlust than piety. Traveling to Canterbury, they stopped along the roadsides to entertain listeners. Two tales were told by each pilgrim on the way to Canterbury and two on the return journey. Thirty travelers, not including the Host and Canon's Yeoman, supposedly created these tales, and more than 124 of them were composed. Only about twenty-four of them have survived, and many of these are in fragments. Canterbury, located in Kent in southeastern England, was a major English shrine, and the city had many inns and hostels for pilgrims as well as churches and religious houses.

Excerpts from Chaucer's Tales

Excerpts from *The Canterbury Tales* have been adapted and edited by Anne Malcolmson in the previously mentioned book, *A Taste of Chaucer.* One of the characters in "The Prologue" is the Pardoner. He was a clergyman who was authorized by the Pope to sell indulgences or forgiveness for sins not yet committed. Many false pardoners sold indulgences and pocketed the money. Pardoners usually carried relics of saints such as bones, bits of clothing, or some other object supposedly involved in a miracle. In "The Prologue," Chaucer describes a yellow-haired pardoner with a wallet lying in his lap "stuffed full of pardons bought from Rome."

Later, in "The Pardoner's Tale," Chaucer creates a story with a background of the Black Death or London plagues. Plagues carried by rodents ravaged England in 1361, 1362, and 1369. This is almost an allegorical tale of Death depicted as a sneaking thief who easily slays a thousand persons during a pestilence. Three roisterers, with the help of an aged man, discover florins of pure gold under a tree. The three brawlers quarrel, and one of them rushes to an apothecary shop for poison in order to get rid of his fellow scoundrels and seize the treasure for himself.

This same tale appears in an adaptation, "The Three Young Men and Death," translated and adapted by Jennifer Westwood in a book titled *Medieval Tales* (Coward-McCann). Other tales in this adaptation are "The Tale of Chanticleer," "The Loathly Lady," "The Devil and the Summoner," and "The Alchemist."

Chaucer is significant in the story of language miracles because he was the first great poet of the English language and one of the most gifted storytellers of all time. In Chaucer's time, French was the language of law and of the King, but English was spoken by most Londoners. This was known as Middle English, a combination of French and Anglo-Saxon.

Other Tales of the Middle Ages

Another story of fourteenth century England describing the Black Plague is *The Door in the Wall* by Marguerite de Angeli (Doubleday & Co.). Robin is the crippled son of Sir John de Bureford. His father goes to the Scottish war and his mother works in the Queen's household. Robin, crippled by a strange malady at the time of the plague, is educated by Brother Luke, who teaches him that reading is "a door in the wall." This book is beautifully illustrated by the author.

A novel which also depicts a yearning for knowledge is *A Candle at Dusk* by E. M. Almedingen (Farrar, Straus & Giroux). The setting of this story is laid in an eighth century Frankish kingdom.

Young Idrun, the son of a wealthy landowner, spends his early life with other boys doing farming tasks and fighting with bows and arrows, pikes, and axes. One day he visits the library at Ligugé and is seized with an overpowering desire to learn reading and writing from the monks there. His father, Berno, an unlettered man, opposes his son's desire to learn his letters at the monastary, because he, Berno, has been having a feud with the monks of the abbey who are trying to take over his property through the use of forged parchment documents and corrupt law courts. It is not until Idrun heroically kills a wild boar which is threatening the life of a serving woman that he is granted any wish he desires. His wish is to learn to read and write. The boy feels that reading is like a bird set free to fly through the skies. Books of this period are sheets of parchment sewn together, with wooden boards as covers. The "Book of Lights," a collection of quotations laboriously copied by Dom Defensor, becomes the most significant book in Idrun's life, and studying with the learned monk is like windows opening new vistas, to a boy starved for book knowledge. The boy learns secrets about the preparation of ink and parchment, and he learns about using "contractions" to eliminate vowels in order to save space on parchment pages.

Almedingen writes of this early period of Frankish history with colorful details presented in a vivid manner. Characterizations of the father and mother, Berno and Aldis, of Idrun and Judith are presented in a setting of much strife, a time when the Saracens are threatening to destroy Poitiers in the year 732. The author was born in Russia, but she is now a British subject and has also published *The Young Leonardo da Vinci, Russian Folk and Fairy Tales,* and *Young Mark* (Farrar, Straus & Giroux), a prize book in Book World's 1968 Spring Festival.

A small book for young children is *Books a Book to Begin On* by Susan Bartlett (Holt, Rinehart & Winston). This little volume is descriptively illustrated by Ellen Raskin. It tells many interesting facts such as, for example, the use of tied knots on strings by Incas, the use of *rune staves* by the Scandinavians, and the development of the stylus in India for *Brahmi Script* written on bark strips. A pictorial illustration shows monks at work on their pictures or *illuminations* and includes the famous illuminated Irish manuscript, the *Book of Kells,* which is more than 1300 years old.

The significance of lithography in the history of printing is depicted in *Printing from Stone, the Story of Lithography* by S. Carl Hirsch (The Viking Press). Lithography probably originated from ancient stone rubbings formed more than a thousand years ago. The Field Museum of Natural History has a stone rubbing made in the year 1107 and inscribed with an image of Confucius. In 1798, Aloys Senefelder developed a practical method of making a lithograph from drawings on smooth limestone. He later wrote a book, *A Complete Course of Lithography.* The Hirsch volume discusses the value of the lithographic process in portraying caricatures and political cartoons by Honore Daumier, as well as in lithographing the tremendous number of Currier and Ives prints. The significance of a Lincoln picture, based on Brady's photograph taken in 1860, is also depicted in an interesting way.

Two volumes by Christine Price, *Made in the Middle Ages* and *Made in the Renaissance* (E. P. Dutton & Co.), add valuable information about the cultural life, as well as the arts and crafts, of each of those historic periods.

Made in the Middle Ages includes a chapter "Books for the Church." During the latter part of the twelfth century, at the time of the Third Crusade, an artist created a beautiful initial B for the first page of a Psalter. At this time, monks laboriously copied many of the books of the world in a scriptorium or writing room. During the earlier part of the Middle Ages, books were preserved in the monasteries and were so valuable that they were heavily chained to prevent their removal. In fact, a book cost almost as much as a home. Capital initials were beautifully designed and painstakingly illustrated on parchment documents. Gradually, a process of grinding gold leaf to a powder and attaching it to the parchment with glues made of egg or of boiled scraps of vellum was developed. Artist creators of miniatures to adorn royal robes also designed pictures for elaborate embroidered church vestments.

Tales of the Renaissance Period

The second volume by Christine Price, *Made in the Renaissance,* Arts and Crafts of the Age of Exploration (E. P. Dutton & Co.), contains an interesting chapter, "Books and Printing," as well as many other pages about craftsmen, clothing and textiles, weapons, furniture, sculpture, musical instruments, and navigation. The chapter about printing discusses the style of print used in the Gutenberg Bible published in Mainz, Germany in 1456. The author also describes the exquisite craftsmanship of Aldus Manutius, a Venetian printer, who published famous pocket-size volumes of Latin classics for scholars. Brief mention is made of the first printed Book of Hours developed by a Parisian wood engraver, Philip Pigouchet. This is a book of prayers which includes prayers for various hours of the day. It has exquisitely designed miniatures and borders in brilliant blue, red, and gold.

The Renaissance was an historical period when resplendently beautiful tapestries were designed and woven for vain rulers such as Henry VIII of England and Francis I of France who desired splendor in their personal robes and in the royal hangings.

One of the most magnificent historical cloth pieces was the Bayeaux tapestry. The tale of this great cloth masterpiece is told in *The Bayeaux Tapestry*, the Story of the Norman Conquest, 1066, by Norman Denny and Josephine Filmer-Sankey (Atheneum Publishers). This book consists almost entirely of reproductions of panels of the famous tapestry which is more than 230 feet long and twenty inches wide. The cloth proclaims in picture the glories of the Norman Conquest of England and the dramatic events leading up to the famous battle between Harold Godwissom of Essex and William of Normandy. Actually, this cloth painting should not be called a tapestry as it is not woven on a loom. It is, rather, a piece of embroidery or needlework which has pictures stitched in colored woolen threads extending across a long strip of bleached linen.

Kenneth M. Setton who authored a fascinating article, "The Norman Conquest," which appeared in *National Geographic* magazine dated August, 1966, reviews some difficulties encountered in preserving this historical relic. The tapestry appeared in an inventory of the Cathedral of Bayeaux in 1476. More than three centuries later, in 1792, some French revolutionaries almost destroyed it by using it as a wagon cover. In 1794, it was almost cut up to decorate a float. During World War II, it was wound around a huge spool and hidden in a cellar of the Louvre. A former bishops' palace across from the Bayeaux Cathedral now displays this famous embroidery, and special lighting is used to preserve its colors. Visitors can view the tapestry and listen to recorded commentaries as they look at such scenes as William's invasion or a fleet sailing for England. Children reading *The Bayeaux Tapestry* can relive an ancient historical era when men fought in armor, falcons at their wrists, or when they sailed in ships resembling colorful Viking vessels.

A recent novel for older children about the Norman Conquest is *Banner Over Me* by Margery P. Greenleaf, which is illustrated by Charles Mikolaycek (Follett Publishing Co.). This story depicts the historical period immediately before and immediately after the Norman invasion. The plot concerns two Saxons, twin brothers, who are engulfed in the epic conflict between King Harold of England and William, Duke of Normandy.

Teachers may want to use *Now I Remember,* A Holiday History of Britain, (London: Chatto and Windlus) as background for study of the period of Norman architecture which was popular from 1066 until 1189 in England. This book offers a concise history of England and includes many pictures.

Two other books for children about the Norman Conquest are *1066* by Franklin Hamilton (Dial Press), and *The Norman Conquest,* written and illustrated by C. Walter Hodges (Coward-McCann). An interesting book by Bernice Grohskopf concerning manuscripts and writing is *From Age to Age,* Life and Literature in Anglo-Saxon England, (Atheneum Publishers). This volume consists of translations of prose from the old English period, 500 to the year 1066. It includes excerpts from Beowulf and information on charms and diseases. Photographs reconstruct Anglo-Saxon history from manuscripts. Much information is given on the making of manuscripts at the time when monks laboriously worked in carrels or cubicles.

The Norman conquest was significant in the history of language as the use of English and the Anglo-Saxon tongue declined, and Latin and French became popular in church, state, and high society functions. English became the language of the country people and was principally spoken by the common man in his home or at the pub.

Books about Language History

Two other books which dramatically depict some miracles of language history are: *The Wonderful World of Communication* by Lancelot Hogben (Garden City Books), and *The Language Book* by Franklin Folsom (Grosset & Dunlap). The Hogben volume discusses ancient temple observatories and accurate calendars developed by the Mayas. It portrays the countries of Mesopotamia where writers punched symbols on slabs of clay, and Egypt where papyrus was used extensively. An indebtedness to Oriental writing is outlined, and pictures of two syllabaries, the Katakana and Hiragana, are reproduced. Hogben also traces the contributions of Semitic Phoenicians who distributed the idea of letters in the Mediterranean World before 600 B.C. In a chapter, "Penman to Printer," the author outlines some developmental steps in printing which are beautifully illustrated with pages from the Wycliffe Bible, wood-block printing, and illuminated letters designed by skilled goldsmiths and armorers. Other chapters discuss the history of the motion picture, telegraph, and television.

The Language Book by Folsom includes data on the progress of language from its early beginnings to the idea of an international language such as Esperanto or Kosmos. Many interesting aspects of language history are illustrated by John Hull and Tran Mawicke. The detective work of Jean-François Champollion is described in picture and prose. Language family trees such as one on Indo-European languages are also described and illustrated. One of the most interesting chapters in this Folsom volume is titled "How to Make a Language." This includes skills such as attaching sounds to desired meanings, combining portions of old words into new ones, borrowing terms from other languages, and inventing new words to meet a situation. For example, Folsom mentions the African Hausa tribe who describe the malaria-infested mosquito as "It-Keeps-the-White-Men-Out."

Numerous alphabet books will be discussed in the activities of this chapter, but *Beasts: An Alphabet of Fine Prints* by Catherine L.

Fuller (Little, Brown and Co.) is related to the story of birds and stones. This book contains twenty-six animal prints which are arranged and lettered alphabetically. Reproductions and engravings, etchings, woodcuts, and lithographs illustrate the text and introduce the artistry of graphic art. Some criteria for selection of prints are artistic style, technical excellence, suitability, clarity of detail, and compatibility of design.

This chapter offers only a glimpse of language history, commencing with pictographs and ancient hieroglyphs portraying the ibis and the eagle and progressing to falconry and colorful lithographs of animal figures carved or etched in stone. This form of history is still being written; an article in a recent newspaper announced that fifteen lines of poetry authored by Ovid had been found etched in stone atop a column of ruins at Sulmona, the site of the ancient poet's home near Rome.

Pupils can make numerous exciting explorations in language history. Some activities relating to this chapter follow.

Enrichment Ideas Related to Language

THE WONDERFUL ALPHABET

Some Activities for Young Children

An Alphabet Fair: A large number of ABC books have been designed by notable artists, including the *Lear Alphabet ABC* (McGraw-Hill Book Co.); Fritz Eichenberg's *Ape in a Cape* (Harcourt, Brace & World); and Wanda Gág's *ABC Bunny* (Coward-McCann). Other attractive alphabet books include *Bruno Munari's ABC* (Atheneum Publishers). *Add-a-Line Alphabet* by Don Freeman (Golden Gate Junior Books) and *Alphabet of Puppy Care* by Lisl Weil (Abelard-Schuman) are also interesting. The teacher might suggest having an Alphabet Book Fair and ask primary grade children to bring favorite alphabet books to share.

Making Alphabet Trees: Leo Lionni has written and illustrated a delightful book, *The Alphabet Tree* (Pantheon Books), which is an informative story for children in preschool and primary grade classes. The tale commences with letters of the alphabet clinging to beautiful leaves in gusts of wind. Along comes a brightly colored word bug who teaches them to join together to form words. Next appears a lavender caterpillar who advises them that sentences have more meaning than mere words. The caterpillar persuades the letters to join together to become words in a sentence offering a significant message.

1. An alphabet tree for a bulletin board can be constructed, with the letters of the alphabet dangling from the twigs. The letters can be sprinkled with glitter and sequins, or they can be painted in brilliant colors.
2. A flannelgraph picture of an alphabet tree can be created by attaching to a flannelgraph tree numerous letters of the alphabet made from flannelgraph material. This can form the background for playing a Word Bug game in which letters can be regrouped into different combinations to form words. A colorful lavender caterpillar with huge owlish eyes can be made, and he can help the children form meaningful sentences.

Some Activities for Older Children

Calligraphy: Pupils can carefully study the calligraphy of Ogg and design original alphabetic letters, or they can create personified letters in humorous styles.

Creating Original Alphabet Books: Older children can make original alphabet books for younger children. A book such as *The Alphabet Tale* by Jan Garten (Random House) is fun to design. In this volume, an incomplete verse is written with a dash left to indicate a rhyming word that gives a clue as to the name of the animal. For instance, if R is the letter, the verse might be:

> Hoppity-hop, with ears so tall,
> This animal's tail is a fuzzy - - - - -. (ball)

A rabbit can be drawn in such a way that his tail is on one page and his body is on another.

Alliterative Alphabets: An alliterative alphabet is fun for children in the fourth or fifth grades when they have acquired some vocabulary fluency. Marcia Brown has created a different type of ABC book, *Peter Piper's Alphabet,* subtitled Peter Piper's Practical Principles of Plain and Perfect Pronunciations, (Charles Scribner's Sons). Lines of verse are printed as nonsensical tongue twisters. Such a book can be illustrated with magazine pictures or by the use of letters cut from finger painted paper. Considerable dexterity with a dictionary or synonym book is needed in order to compose couplets or quatrains in a tongue twister style.

Word Woman Vocabulary Game: In *Catch Me a Wind* by Patricia Hubbell (Atheneum Publishers) appears an unusual poem, "The Word Woman," which tells about an old woman with silver hair who carries a jar containing interesting words. After reading the poem, children may be motivated to play a game. One child plays the part of the old woman. Other pupils write exciting words on colored slips of paper and place them in her jar. On Word Woman Day, each child draws a word out of the jar, reads it, and uses it in a phrase or a sentence.

Making Original Abecedarian Books: Older pupils will enjoy creating an original abecedarian book similar to *The Abecedarian Book* by Charles W. Ferguson (Little, Brown and Co.). The words to be used are, for the most part, unusual multisyllabic ones such as "antediluvian," "bioluminescent," and "cacophony."

ACTIVITIES RELATED TO PRINTING AND LITHOGRAPHY

Biography of Gutenberg: Criteria for good biographies should be developed. Intermediate grade children who are studying the biographical genre might be asked to take research notes on scattered bits of information about Johann Gutenberg. Then a brief biographical sketch might be written.

Potato and Linoleum Prints: Potato or linoleum block prints can be designed and used to illustrate the principle of printing.

Pressblock Printing: A newer commercial media is *Pressblock,* a patented device in which no cutting tools are used, to form the relief image. Child artists draw with a soft pencil or a ballpoint pen on a cellular plastic face, and lines are sharply outlined. The Pressblock is inked with textile dyes, temperas, or acrylic paints. A brayer or roller is rolled over the design and it is transferred to paper. Information is available from Durable Arts, Box 2413, San Rafael, California 94901.

Crayon Rubbings: After studying pictures of rubbings depicted in *Printing from a Stone, the Story of Lithography,* pupils may wish to make rubbings. Paper can be placed over leaves, gravel, or small objects to make interesting patterns. Younger primary age children will enjoy several tactile experiences suggested by Ann Kirn in *Full of Wonder* (World Publishing Co.) An unusual book for adults is *Gyotaku; the Art and Technique of the Japanese Fish Print* (University of Washington Press), which describes the principle of early fish rubbings.

BAYEAUX TAPESTRY ACTIVITIES

Reading and Reporting Related Literature Books: Intermediate grade pupils may be asked to read a novel which is somewhat related to the pictorial scenes in the historically oriented piece of embroidery, the Bayeaux Tapestry. *The Keys and the Candle* by Maryhale Woolsey (Abingdon Press) begins its story in the year 1001. There is a chapter, "A Sign from the Sky," which deals with falconry. After reading this chapter, a pupil may consult an encyclopedia and other sources to learn more about falconry, or to study about knighthood, serfdom, illuminated manuscripts, King Alfred of England, or the scriptorium.

Writing a Tapestry Narrative: The teacher or pupils may find in a secondhand book store or at some other outlet which handles back issues of the National Geographic magazine, the August, 1966 copy which contains an article, "The Norman Conquest" by Kenneth M. Setton. After studying the historical events portrayed in the Bayeaux embroidery masterpiece, the pupils may write the story of the tapestry in a narrative style. The same procedure may be followed with the book, *The Bayeaux Tapestry*, by Norman Denny and Josephine Filmer-Sankey.

(While not directly related to the Bayeaux Tapestry, the two following activities are mentioned here because they do involve the arts of stitchery and rug or tapestry making.)

Creative Stitchery Art Activities: Intermediate grade children who are studying United States history can create an original piece of historical embroidery depicting famous events of our country's history. Leadership in the classroom is necessary in order to embellish significant historical events. Committees can be formed, events outlined, and strips of paper assembled somewhat on the order of a time-line pictograph. In this way, a pattern for embroidery work can be designed.

Creative Stitchery and Language
by Lynn M. Johnson
Cal-State College,
Hayward, California

The most effective pictures can be selected and transferred to cloth. A recent book, *Stitchery for Children,* A Manual for Teachers, Parents, and Children, by Jacqueline Enthoven (Reinhold Publishing Corp.) has numerous suggestions for creative stitchery projects, with illustrations of various stitcheries accomplished by boys and girls at different age levels, from two-and-a-half years through high school. The second chapter describes stitches and variations. The third chapter discusses the use of color and also some children's stitchery murals which are projects enjoyed by the ten-to-twelve-year-olds. An example is given of an "Alice in Wonderland" sampler which had been designed and executed by children in the Potomac School in McLean, Virginia. To make an original piece of embroidery, drawings are traced on layout paper. Each pupil has a piece of linen, twelve by twelve inches, and some dressmaker's carbon. The linen is taped to their desks, and the designs are transferred to it. Twenty different panels can be created and later sewn together. An earlier book by Mrs. Enthoven, *The Stitches of Creative Embroidery,* discusses an embroidered story of the Norman conquest of England.

Hooked Rugs and Wool Pictures: A more difficult and lengthy project in creating rugs or tapestries is possible if children have stable enough interests to pursue a project for an extensive period of time. Details concerning such a project appear in *Rags, Rugs and Wool Pictures,* A First Book of Rug Hooking, by Ann Wiseman (Charles Scribner's Sons). This book shows some simple designs suggested by patterns in nature, as well as some photographs of hooked pictures created by boys and girls. The author makes various references to early printing, and often mentions "The Book of Hours" with its beautiful illlustrations of the columbine and other flowers. The illustrations also include some of the border pictures which are part of the Bayeaux Tapestry. These scenes show odd creatures representing mythological divinities and animals. Such simple designs of flowers and animals are effective in hand or punchhooked pictures created by young children today.

PROJECTS RELATED TO LANGUAGE BOOKS

The following list of projects may be related to almost any language book which gives some etymological history of language or any information concerning work done to improve language either by linguists, semanticists, anthropologists, or English language specialists.

Rebus Stories: Simple picture writing tales can be created in rebus style.

Tower of Babel Research: *The Tower of Babel* by William Wiesner (The Viking Press) tells the story of Noah after the flood, of the building of the high tower at Babel, and the subsequent loss of communication among the people because the workmen hired to build the tower spoke many different tongues. In the classroom, further research on the story of the Tower of Babel can be conducted. The pupils can dramatize or reenact the problem situations which could arise if various types of jobs today were to be performed under the difficulties arising from lack of communication because many different languages were spoken among the workers.

Symbols in Literature: The significance of the symbol in both literature and advertising can be developed. For instance, Mercury, who was the messenger of the gods, is used by florists; and a particular type of shell is symbolized in a national oil company's advertisements. Children can collect important symbols from magazines and newspapers.

Making Linguistic Word Maps: Portions of *American English* by Albert H. Marckwardt (Oxford University Press) can, with the aid of the teacher, be interpreted through the use of charts or an overhead

Magnetic Board and Linguistic Map
by Joan Cannon
Cal-State College,
Hayward, California

projector. Pupils can use an opaque projector to make outlines of a larger map of the United States. Original symbols can be used to represent English, French, Dutch, German, and Spanish explorers, and these can be placed on areas of the maps where various settlers lived.

Creating Language for an Imaginary Country: An imaginery country in some remote part of the world can be created and a language can be originated for the people.

Creating Multisyllabic Words: Pupils can learn to create big words by combining parts of other words into a large word in a meaningful manner.

International Languages and World Understanding (Creating Dialogues): Pupils can do research on the United Nations and learn more about the significance of language in developing better world understanding. If children are studying Spanish or French, two pupils should work as partners and prepare dialogues. One will speak English and the other will speak the foreign language. Class listeners can compare expressions and fluency.

Geographic Place Names: Children can become interested in the origin of geographical place names. They can interview realtors and older citizens to learn the origin of street names. For instance, San Lorenzo, California has numerous street signs relating to Spanish settlers; and Orinda, California has a section called Sleepy Hollow which has streets named after characters in "The Legend of Sleepy Hollow" by Washington Irving.

Making Foreign Words Menus: Albert H. Marckwardt's *American English* (Oxford University Press) and *General Language, English and Its Foreign Relations* by Lilly Linquist and Clarence Wachner (Holt, Rinehart & Winston), include lists of foods which were named by persons in various countries, as well as by the American Indians. Children can design original menus with the bill-of-fare showing contributions from as many different countries as possible. Also, pupils enjoy writing creative paragraphs which utilize words from at least ten different languages. Members of the class can collect menus from restaurants featuring foreign foods, and they can make lists of names of foreign dishes. Many recipe books which have names for foods written in various languages are available. Samples of some of these foods can be brought to class, with labels or names of the foods carefully printed in manuscript writing.

Creating an Artificial Language: After reading the section "Artificial Language" appearing in the Linquist and Wachner volume men-

Cartoons to illustrate Homonyms
Television Committee in New English
Students taught by
Ruth K. Carlson

tioned before, pupils can study some of the principles of the Esperanto language. Nouns, adjectives, and verbs can be created in Esperanto.

Word Magic Scrapbooks: Pupils can construct original scrapbooks titled "Word Magic" or "Adventures with Words." Materials for the scrapbooks can be taken from magazines and newspaper articles, billboard advertisements, and radio and television programs.

Creating a "Book of Lights": Pupils can create a "Book of Lights" similar to the compilation of quotations made by the monk in *A Candle at Dusk* by Almedingen. The teacher can suggest a few special quotations or phrases, and the children can collect significant statements from literature and from newspapers and magazines. These books can be a long-term project. Covers can be wooden ones decorated by wood burning, or with screen, linoleum, potato, or polystyrene block printing. Some pages could be decorated with collage work. Suggested sources on techniques are *Introducing Textile Printing* by Nora Proud (P. T. Botsford and Watson-Guptill Publications), and *Textile Printing and Painting Made Easy* by Ursula Keuhnemann (Taplinger Publishing Co.). One little book, *Collage,* by Mickey Klar Marks (Dial Press), offers suggestions and illustrations on collage art work.

Crossword Puzzles on Historical Terms: Many words appearing in *A Candle at Dusk* are important vocabulary words such as abbey, monk, parchment, Saracens, Franks, Poitiers, Charlemagne, trestle, caldron, coppice, prior, hospice, chalice, cloister, pallet, papyrus, style (for writing), porter, lectern, vespers, harebill, campion, Byzantium, pilgrim, villein, rushes, braggart, faggot, tripod, novice, culinary, brazier. The teacher and a committee of pupils can create a modified crossword puzzle using these words and others.

A vast world of exploration into the uncharted world of language awaits the modern child standing at the threshold of newer discoveries in language lore. Another approach to language will appear in the next chapter which will include many fantasy adventures with words. Teachers and pupils may wish to consult some of the following sources for background material on some original interpretations of language.

SELECTED REFERENCES FOR CHILDREN

ALMEDINGEN, E. M. *A Candle at Dusk.* New York: Farrar, Straus & Giroux, Inc., 1969.

BARTLETT, SUSAN. *Books A Book to Begin On.* Illustrated by Ellen Raskin. New York: Holt, Rinehart & Winston, Inc., 1968.

BROWN, MARCIA. *Peter Piper's Alphabet.* New York: Charles Scribner's Sons, 1959.

COONEY, BARBARA, ed. *Chanticleer and the Fox.* Illustrated by Barbara Cooney. New York: Thomas Y. Crowell Company, 1959.

DENNY, NORMAN, and FILMER-SANKEY, JOSEPHINE. *The Bayeaux Tapestry Story of the Norman Conquest, 1066.* New York: Atheneum Publishers, 1966.

EICHENBERG, FRITZ. *Ape in a Cape.* New York: Harcourt, Brace & World, Inc., 1952.

FERGUSON, CHARLES W. *The Abecedarian Book.* Boston: Little, Brown and Company, 1964.

FOLSOM, FRANKLIN. *The Language Book.* New York: Grosset & Dunlap, Inc., 1963.

FREEMAN, DON. *Add-a-Line Alphabet.* Los Angeles: Golden Gate Junior Books, 1968.

GÁG, WANDA. *ABC Bunny.* New York: Coward-McCann, Inc., 1933.

GARTEN, JAN. *The Alphabet Tale.* New York: Random House, Inc., 1964.

GROHSKOPF, BERNICE. *From Age to Age,* Life and Literature in Anglo-Saxon England. New York: Antheneum Publishers, 1968.

HAMILTON, FRANKLIN, *1066.* Illustrated by Judith Ann Lawrence. New York: The Dial Press, Inc., 1964.

HARNETT, CYNTHIA. *Caxton's Challenge.* Illustrated by Cynthia Harnett. Cleveland: The World Publishing Company, 1960.

HODGES, C. WALTER. *The Norman Conquest.* Illustrated by C. Walter Hodges. New York: Coward-McCann, Inc., 1966.

HOGBEN, LANCELOT T. *The Wonderful World of Communication.* New York: Garden City Books, 1959.

HUBBELL, PATRICIA. *Catch Me a Wind.* Drawings by Susan Trommler. New York: Atheneum Publishers, 1968.

KIRN, ANN. *Full of Wonder.* Cleveland: The World Publishing Company, 1959.

LEAR, EDWARD. *Alphabet ABC.* New York: McGraw-Hill Book Company, 1965.

LIONNI, LEO. *The Alphabet Tree.* Illustrated by Leo Lionni. New York: Pantheon Books, Inc., 1968.

MALCOLMSON, ANNE. *A Taste of Chaucer.* Illustrated by Enrico Arno. New York: Harcourt, Brace & World, Inc., 1964.

McNeer, May Yonge. *Martin Luther.* Illustrated by Lynd Ward. Nashville: Abingdon Press, 1953.

————. *John Wesley.* Illustrated by Lynd Ward. Nashville: Abingdon Press, 1951.

Mirsky, Reba Paeff. *Brahms.* Illustrated by W. T. Mars. Chicago: Follett Publishing Company, 1966.

————. *Haydn.* Illustrated by W. T. Mars. Chicago: Follett Publishing Company, 1963.

Munari, Bruno. *Bruno Munari's ABC.* Cleveland: The World Publishing Company, 1960.

Neurath, Marie, and Ellis, John. *They Lived Like This in Chaucer's England.* New York: Franklin Watts, Inc., 1967.

Piatti, Celestino. *Piatti's Animal ABC.* New York: Atheneum Publishers, 1966.

Price, Christine. *Made in the Middle Ages.* New York: E. P. Dutton & Co., Inc., 1961.

————. *Made in the Renaissance.* New York: E. P. Dutton & Co., Inc., 1963.

Ripley, Elizabeth. *Leonardo da Vinci.* New York: Henry Z. Walck, Inc., 1952.

————. *Michelangelo.* New York: Henry Z. Walck, Inc., 1953.

Serraillier, Ian. *Chaucer and His World.* New York: Henry Z. Walck, Inc., 1968.

Weil, Lisl. *Alphabet of Puppy Care.* New York: Abelard-Schuman Limited, 1968.

Westwood, Jennifer, translated and adapted by. *Medieval Tales.* Illustrated by Pauline Baynes. New York: Coward-McCann, Inc., 1968.

Wiesner, William. *The Tower of Babel.* New York: The Viking Press, Inc., 1968.

Wildsmith, Brian. *Brian Wildsmith's ABC.* New York: Atheneum Publishers, 1966.

Woolsey, Maryhale. *The Keys and the Candle.* Nashville: Abingdon Press, 1963.

SELECTED REFERENCES FOR PROFESSIONALS AND ADULTS

Alexander, Henry. *The Story of Our Language.* New York: Dolphin, 1962 edition.

Asimov, Isaac. *Words on the Map.* New York: Houghton Mifflin Company, 1962.

Enthoven, Jacqueline. *Stitchery for Children,* A Manual for Teachers, Parents and Children. New York: Reinhold Publishing Corp., 1968.

Fuller, Catherine L. *Beasts: An Alphabet of Fine Prints.* Boston: Little, Brown and Company, 1968.

Girsdansky, Michael. *The Adventure of Language.* Englewood Cliffs, N. J.: Prentice-Hall, Inc., 1963.

Hirsch, S. Carl. *Printing from Stone, the History of Lithography.* New York: The Viking Press, Inc., 1967.

Hiyama, Yoshio. *Gyotaku;* The Art and Technique of the Japanese Fish Print. Seattle: University of Washington Press, 1964.

Keuhnemann, Ursula. *Textile Printing and Painting Made Easy.* New York: Taplinger Publishing Co., Inc., 1967.

LINDQUIST, LILLY, and WACHNER, CLARENCE. *General Language, English and Its Foreign Relations.* New York: Holt, Rinehart & Winston, Inc., 1962.

MARCKWARDT, ALBERT H. *American English.* New York: Oxford University Press, Inc., 1958.

MARKS, MICKEY KLAR. *Collage.* Collage by Edith Alberts. Photos by David Rosenfeld. New York: The Dial Press, Inc., 1968.

Now I Remember, A Holiday History of Britain. London: Chatto & Windlus, 1965.

OGG, OSCAR. *The 26 Letters.* Illustrated by Oscar Ogg. New York: Thomas Y. Crowell Company, 1961.

PROUD, NORA. *Introducing Textile Printing.* New York: and London: P. T. Botsford and Watson-Guptill Publications, 1968.

SETTON, KENNETH M. "The Norman Conquest." *National Geographic,* August, 1966.

SHEARD, J. A. *The Words of English.* New York: W. W. Norton, 1966.

SPARKE, WILLIAM. *The Story of English Language.* Illustrated by Wayne Gallup and with photography. New York: Abelard-Schuman Limited, 1965.

WISEMAN, ANN. *Rags, Rugs and Wool Pictures.* A First Book of Rug Hooking. New York: Charles Scribner's Sons, 1968.

chapter 2

the wonderland of words

Books about Words

Devotees of Charles L. Dodgson savor the nonsensical stories of *Alice in Wonderland* and *Through the Looking-Glass* and relish his clever facility with the English language. This quiet, eccentric mathematician, writing under the pseudonym of Lewis Carroll, mesmerizes the attention of children and adults alike and gently opens imaginative doors to the wonderland of words.

It was on a hot summer day on July 4, 1862. Dodgson had been entertaining Dean Liddell's three daughters Edith, Lorina, and Alice. He took their photographs, and then he and his friend from Trinity College, Robinson Duckworth, rowed the three girls up the river to Godstow. The blazing sun exhausted them, and they wandered over the meadows for shelter near some haycocks. Here in the shimmering sunshine, most of *Alice's Adventures Underground* were told to an eager audience. Alice Liddell was an enthralled listener and begged Dodgson to write the story down so that she could read it again. By February 10, 1863, Lewis Carroll recorded in his diary that the fairy tale, *Alice's Adventures Underground,* was finished but that the illustrations were incomplete. A facsimile page of this manuscript with his own illustrations appears in *Three Centuries of Children's Books in Europe* by Bettina Hürlimann and translated and edited by Brian W. Alderson (The World Publishing Co.). Later, Carroll commissioned John Tenniel to illustrate his volume which was published by The Macmillan Company. Tenniel enhanced the grotesque ideas of the tales and made them more understandable to others.

Numerous editions of this classic have been published. One of these, by the Washington Square Press, is titled *Alice in Wonderland and Other Favorites,* with ninety-two illustrations by Sir John Tenniel, the original artist. This inexpensive paperback includes *Alice's Adventures in Wonderland, Through the Looking-Glass,* and *The Hunting of the Snark.* The first tale was published in 1865, and *Through the Looking-Glass and What Alice Found There* appeared in 1871. A little poem written as a preface to this latter volume speaks of the child of "pure unclouded brow and dreaming eyes of wonder!" At the end of this story, there is another poem in which the initial letters of each line, when read downward, spell out the full name of the original Alice, A-L-I-C-E P-L-E-A-S-A-N-C-E L-I-D-D-E-L-L. Carroll reconstructs the hot, sunny evening in July and speaks of a wonderland where golden dreams occupy children with eager eyes and willing ears. Those who wish to know Carroll better may want to read "Lewis Carroll" in *Tellers of Tales,* British Authors of Children's Books from 1800 to 1964, by Roger Lancelyn Green (Franklin Watts, Inc.).

Most persons are familiar with the basic story line of *Alice in Wonderland.* Alice is sitting on a river bank, bored and inattentive, until she meets the White Rabbit who is worrying about being late as he pulls his watch from his waistcoat pocket. Intrigued by the Rabbit, she follows him across the field and falls down a rabbit hole. She lands in a strange place where different liquids and foods cause her size to change many times, and the world becomes "curiouser and curiouser." She meets many odd creatures, the Lory, the Dodo, the Eaglet, the Duchess, and most nonsensical of all is the Queen who often orders her subjects to chop off someone's head. The grinning Cheshire-Cat offers advice, and Alice suddenly finds herself at a Mad Tea Party. She has fantastic adventures with the March Hare, the Hatter, and the Dormouse. Some strange conversations ensue but which, nevertheless, have some logical roots. When the March Hare invites Alice to have more tea, she petulantly replies that she can't take more as she has had nothing yet. The Hatter informs her that she can't take *less,* and that it is easier "to take *more* than nothing."

Alice is surprised when she sees the Queen's croquet ground. The game is strange in that the balls and mallets are live hedgehogs and flamingoes. Even the soldiers double themselves up and stand on their hands and feet to make arches for the players.

One of the most interesting uses of language in this classic appears in "The Mock Turtle's Story." Here the mad Queen leaves Alice alone with a Gryphon, and the two of them visit the Mock Turtle with his large tear-filled eyes. He says that he went to school to an old Turtle called the Tortoise. When Alice asks him why he is called a tortoise if he isn't one, the Mock Turtle angrily replies that it is because he "taught us." (Washington Square Press Edition, p. 84.) Then the Mock Turtle explains his school curriculum which consists of "Reeling and

Writhing . . . . . and the different branches of Arithmetic—Ambition, Distraction, Uglification, and Derision." (Washington Square Press Edition, p. 85.) When Alice challenges the Turtle by saying that she has never heard of "uglification," the Gryphon acts surprised and asks her if she hasn't heard of "beautify." This leaves Alice to draw her own relationships between the two words.

Other courses in the Mock Turtle's curriculum are "Mystery, ancient and modern, with Seaography; then Drawling" which is taught by a conger-eel who teaches "Drawling, Stretching, and Fainting in Coils." The Turtle explains that he went to school ten hours the first day, nine hours the next, and so on. When Alice thinks this is curious, the Gryphon remarks, "That's the reason they're called lessons, because they lessen from day to day." (Washington Square Press Edition, p. 86.)

In the second Carroll tale, Alice steps through a mirror to a Looking-Glass World where things seem backward and strange. This is the land of chess where one meets the Red King and Queen, the White King and Queen, and other chess figures. Here Alice reads the much quoted poem, "Jabberwocky," which is probably the best piece of literature in the English language to teach structure and syntax of grammar. It uses nonsense words such as *brillig, slithy toves,* and the *frumious Bandersnatch.* Alice enters a garden of live flowers and converses with the tiger lilies, daisies, and some looking-glass insects. Here she sees a "rocking-horse-fly" which is bright and sticky, a "snapdragon-fly," and a "bread-and-butter-fly." She meets Tweedledum and Tweedledee and sympathizes with the oysters in "The Walrus and the Carpenter."

The White Queen explains a mysterious life where one is living backwards and memory works both ways. When Alice meets Humpty Dumpty, she knows that she is indeed in a strange world. It is in this chapter, "Humpty Dumpty," that Carroll makes commentaries on language. Humpty Dumpty boasts that his cravat is a present from the White King and Queen and is an "un-birthday present." When Alice asks him about an "un-birthday present," Humpty Dumpty replies that it is a present given when it isn't your birthday. Alice and Humpty Dumpty argue about words, and he scornfully says "When *I* use a word, it means just what I choose it to mean—neither more nor less." (Washington Square Press Edition, p. 190.) Alice replies "The question it whether you *can* make words mean so many different things." (Washington Square Press Edition, p. 190.) Humpty Dumpty explains that some words have a temper. These are usually verbs, which are the proudest ones. Adjectives are more adaptable. He brags that *he* can "manage the whole lot of them." (Washington Square Press Edition, p. 190-191.)

Alice then asks Humpty Dumpty to explain the meaning of words in the first verse of "Jabberwocky." He explains, "*Brillig* means four o'clock in the afternoon—the time when you begin broiling things for dinner," and "*slithy* means 'lithe and slimy.'" He further explains that this is a portmanteau word, one in which two meanings are packed into one. *Toves* are similar to badgers and lizards, and are also like corkscrews. The words *gyre* and *gimble* are explained. *Gyre* means to whirl around like a gyroscope. "To *gimble* is to make holes like a gimlet." "*Mimsy* is 'flimsy and miserable,'" and a *borogove* is a "thin, shabby-looking bird with its feathers sticking out all round—something like a live mop." Alice asks about other words including the meaning of *outgrabe*. Humpty Dumpty explains that *outgrabing* is something between bellowing and whistling, with a kind of sneeze in the middle, (Washington Square Press Edition, p. 193).

Another author of classics, Edward Lear, like Lewis Carroll, also cleverly nurtures the imaginative powers of his readers through his nonsensical use of diction. Although Lear has been credited with originating the limerick, this verse form was actually created by others. *The Oxford Dictionary of Nursery Rhymes,* edited by Iona and Peter Opie, (Oxford at the Clarendon Press), includes a plate illustrating the limerick, "There was a sick man of Tobago." This verse was published in *Anecdotes and Adventures of Fifteen Gentlemen* in 1822 by John Marshall. It was probably illustrated by Robert Cruikshank.

Edward Lear, then, did not invent this poetic form, but he certainly popularized it through both his nonsensical lines and his clever drawings. His "Eight and Forty Nonsense Limericks" have been published in *The Book of Nonsense,* edited by R. L. Green, (E. P. Dutton & Co.). In these verses, one meets, among others, an old man whose beard is a nesting place for two owls and a hen, four larks and a wren. There is also the young lady whose chin is as sharp as a pin, so it is used to pluck the strings of a harp.

Lear has been described as the poet of nonsense. He was born in 1812, twenty years before Lewis Carroll, and he was the twentieth child of Jeremiah Lear. His father was the son of a Danish immigrant and was a wealthy merchant until unfortunate enterprises made him bankrupt. He was held in jail until his wife could pay his many debts. Lear's mother abandoned her twenty children so that she would be free to care for her husband while he was imprisoned. Daily, year after year, she carried a six-course dinner to him in debtor's prison. Many of their children died from neglect. Edward was mothered by his sister, Ann, who was twenty-one years older than he. He studied to be a draughtsman and drew pathological illustrations for doctors. When he was eighteen years of age, he obtained a commission to do drawings of a species of parrot in the London Zoo. This was followed by other commissions until he received an invitation from the Earl of Derby to draw sketches of the animals on his private estate at Knowsley. Here Lear lived for four years during which time he enjoyed visiting with children in the nursery, preferring the company of boys and girls to that of adults.

He created his first book, *A Book of Nonsense*, for these children, and it was published in 1846. Besides his limericks, Lear is known for such narrative verse as "The Owl and the Pussy Cat," "The Jumblies," "The Pobble Who Had No Toes," and "The Quangle-Wangle's Hat." Most of Lear's poetry is lyrical enough to be sung. His words, such as those in "The Courtship of the Yonghy-Bonghy-Bo," actually sing a jingly tune. Professor Pomè of San Remo, Italy arranged this verse for the piano, and a copy of the music appears in *The Complete Nonsense Book* by Edward Lear, edited by Lady Strachey (Dodd, Mead & Co.). Lear also created an alliterative alphabet book, commencing with "The Absolutely Abstemious Ass" and concluding with "The ZigZag Zealous Zebra." His words in "Alphabet" are probably too sophisticated for younger boys and girls, but many children enjoy listening to some of his multisyllabic lines. His "Nonsense Alphabet" in four-line verses is simpler, and more fun for younger children.

Other types of nonsensical verse appear in *Oh What Nonsense!* which has poems selected by William Cole and drawings by Tomi Ungerer (Viking Press). In his introduction to this volume, Cole calls attention to nonsense words which cause laughter, such as "twiddle twaddle," "fiddle faddle," and "balderdash." These are words whose sounds seem to reinforce absurdities in meaning. In "The Folk Who Live in Backward Town," Mary Ann Hoberman describes people who sleep beneath their beds. John Ciardi depicts a weeping man who sings in "The Man in the Onion Bed." Edgar Parker, in "The Contrary Waiter," describes a tarsier waiter who brings food which has not been ordered by his diners. Cole and Ungerer have also collaborated on other fun and nonsense books such as *Frances Face-Maker* (The World Publishing Co.) and *Beastly Boys and Ghastly Girls* (The World Publishing Co.).

Another variety of word wonderland consists of strange situations which arise when words or letters are entangled or missing. A book of this type is *The Wonderful O* by James Thurber which is illustrated by Marc Simont (Simon and Schuster). This is both a fantasy and a satire. It mysteriously commences with a melancholy scene in which Littlejack and Black examine a treasure map and decide to sail in a peculiar ship, the *Aeiu*, which has all of the important vowels but *O*. Strange events occur after Black issues an edict declaring that words in books or signs having an *O* in them will be erased or destroyed. The story utilizes clever situations, as well as words which will enhance the vocabulary development and the imaginative power of children and adults alike.

A recent book for younger children which has somewhat the same theme is *The Night They Stole the Alphabet* by Sesyle Joslin and illustrated by Enrico Arno (Harcourt, Brace & World). In this book, Victoria has many unusual adventures when she hunts for the alphabet letters stolen from her wallpaper and books. She searches for, and finds, the twenty-six letters in strange places. She finds a baby with a B in its bonnet, meets Madame Muzz, and is ordered to mind her P's and Q's. An owl welcomes her to a cup of T. Victoria's adventures are similar to those of Alice in Wonderland, and some of the play on letters reminds one of the Thurber book.

Another modern example of off-beat fantasy which is centered upon a kingdom of words is *The Phantom Tollbooth* by Norton Juster, with illustrations by Jules Feiffer (Random House). In this book, we are introduced to Milo who, bored with his usual school tasks, assembles the Phantom Tollbooth and has numerous strange adventures. He meets such characters as King Azaz the Unabridged, unhappy ruler of Dictionopolis, a mathemagician, Faintly Macabre, and the Watchdog Tock. He searches for Rhyme and Reason and becomes involved in a war between words and numbers, arrives at the Island of Conclusions and even visits the Mountains of Ignorance. This fantasy has enough word wealth to offer activities for a whole semester if children and adults explore it with imaginative thinking games and experiences.

Joan Joy and Marilyn Potter developed a year's program of word study based on The Phantom Tollbooth. Their activities are described in "Dictionopolis" in the April, 1964 issue of *Elementary English.* This article explains how pupils can become citizens of Dictionopolis and buy and sell words in a word market. On the last Friday of the third month, children are given a golden key if they have learned the prescribed number of words. Five booths are built for the word market and are named *The Village of Verbs, Nifty Nouns, Active Adjectives, Adding Adverbs,* and a *Special of the Week.* Various officials of Dictionopolis are the Treasurer of the Word Bank, the Viceroy of Verbs, the Admiral of Adjectives, the Honorable Master of Homonyms, the Secretary of Synonyms, the Attaché of Adverbs, and many others. The "Weekly Specials" are additional fun activities such as one called "Capturing Colors—Riotous Red." During this week, pupils collect descriptive words and phrases related to red, such as fire engine red, magenta red. Another activity. "Arresting Said—Use Another Instead," asks pupils to find substitutes for the word *said* when they are describing conversation in paragraphs or stories.

In addition to books using fantastic situations and nonsensical language, some interest can be aroused in magical words through books which focus upon interesting facts and history about words. One of these is *The First Book of Words,* Their Family History (Franklin Watts). Sam and Beryl Epstein are the authors, and Laszlo Roth did the illustrations. This book is designed for younger children and has information on "Families of Language," "The Beginnings of English," "The Norman Conquest," "Latin and Greek Words," and "How Men First Wrote Their Words." Many interesting details include such information as the origin of the *sandwich* by the Earl of Sandwich, and the *watt* named for the Scottish scientist, James Watt.

A similar book about language for older children is Margaret S. Ernst's *Words, English Roots and How They Grow* (Alfred A. Knopf). This volume suggests many interesting activities to do with words, and it offers some historical data on such words as *etymology.* Historical data is given on the Britons, Anglo-Saxons, and the Jutes, and a description of the Norman Conquest of England is also briefly stated.

Another fascinating book, one which is better for teachers than for students, is *The Magic and Mystery of Words* by J. Donald Adams (Holt, Rinehart & Winston). Adams discusses word nuances and feelings which man has had for certain words such as *dawn* and *dusk.* He reminds readers that innocent sounding words such as *pacification* have covered merciless bombings of defenseless villages. The author describes beautiful words and cites the ones which are considered beautiful by Dr. Wilfred Funk. These include, among others, *golden, cerulean,* and *melody.* Adams points out that some words are beautiful in isolation, while others have beauty in certain combinations. In his fourth chapter entitled "Clichés and Curious Expressions," the author examines such phrases as "keep a stiff upper lip" and "independent as a hog on ice." Some teachers may object to a chapter in this volume entitled "Those Four Letter Words," because certain offending words mentioned here are not usually permitted in books for children. However, these same words can now be published in newspapers and magazines. Interesting data in this volume can be applied to many novel word explorations.

In recent years, several little books have been designed for younger children, books which raise the vocabulary level above that of tired, listless terms. Some of these, such as *Ounce, Dice, Trice* by Alastair Reid (Atlantic Monthly Press, Little, Brown and Co.) offer interesting things to do with words. This book, which is illustrated by Ben Shawn, has amusing sections such as "Squishy Words," on words which give a feeling of wetness, and "Bug Words," which are grumpy ones. One interesting section is entitled "Names for Twins" and includes such double words as "Higgledy-Piggledy," "Namby and Pamby," and "Mumbo and Jumbo." Many delightful language curiosities appear in this little volume.

Another book about words is *Sparkle and Spin* by Ann and Paul Rand (Harcourt, Brace & World). This little volume is beautifully designed and gives examples of onomatopoetic terms, homonyms, and descriptive words. An interesting book illustrating non-verbal language, such as gestures and bodily movement, is *Talking without Words* by Marie Hall Ets (Viking Press).

John Graham has developed the concept *crowd* through a little volume, *A Crowd of Cows*, which is colorfully illustrated by Feodor Rojankovsky, (Harcourt, Brace & World). Another little book for children between the ages of four and seven, one which has been reissued in a smaller format and newer three-color illustrations, is *The B Book* by Phyllis McGinley (Crowell, Collier and Macmillan). A third book which is fun for children from three to seven years, and which has been mentioned in the previous chapter, is *The Alphabet Tree*, written and illustrated in color by Leo Lionni, (Pantheon Books). In this little volume, a word bug points out the significance of letters in words, and a caterpillar teaches the power of words.

Another approach to the creation of original words appears in *From Ambledee to Zumbledee* by Sandol Stoddard Warburg, illustrated by Walter Lorraine, (Houghton Mifflin Co.). In this little book for young children, original words such as "jolly popper" and "slurm" appear. ("Slurm" means to swallow and chew.) A clever publication for young readers is *Would You Put Your Money in a Sand Bank?* Fun with Words, by Harold Longman (Rand McNally & Co.). This book cleverly plays upon differences of words in context, such as "bank of clouds," "riverbank," "snowbank," or "banks of Loch Lomond."

A book of word history designed for young teen-agers is *What's Behind the Word?*, also by Longman, and illustrated by Susan Perl, (Coward-McCann). This gives an account of the origin of thirty-nine English words which are commonly known. Another book for this same age level is *The Story of the English Language* by William Sparke (Abelard-Schuman).

A few books for young children are being published in bilingual or trilingual editions so that pupils can compare English words with their counterparts in other languages. An example of this type of book is *What Do I Say?*, with a story by Norma Simon and pictures by Joe Lasker, (Albert Whitman & Co.). This volume is an English-Spanish edition, planned for the Puerto Rican child. It is designed as a listening book and encourages young children to answer the question "What do I say?" "*Que digo?*" It has simple phrases, and words and questions which are clearly illustrated so that a child's language can be helped through the use of both pictures and simple phrases.

Another example of this type of language book is *At Home: A Visit in Four Languages* (Macmillan Co.), which was written by Esther Hautzig and illustrated by Aliki. It has only thirty-two pages and includes a glossary and a phonetic guide. This is a multilingual picture book in English, French, Spanish, and Russian which gives a feeling of comfort and companionship in family life whether families live in Chicago, Marseilles, Barcelona, or Leningrad. A second book by the same author, but illustrated by Ezra Jack Keats, *In the Park, An Excursion in Four Languages* (Macmillan Co.), introduces parks in New York, Paris, Moscow, and Madrid. Names for familiar things are given in four languages. A pronunciation guide to the Russian alphabet is appended.

The ears of childhood should become attuned to language which is sparkling and fresh, not just to tired-out words and phrases. A little book by Mary Stolz, *Say Something* (Harper & Row, Publishers) uses language beautifully. Fresh, attractive illustrations by Edward Frascino and simple words encourage pupils to say something about the grass, the moon, a tadpole, a mountain, or a tree. Another delightful book is *The Pedaling Man and Other Poems* by Russell Hoban (W. W. Norton & Co.). This volume offers poems for the young child, poems which have the same freshness of language that is found in *Say Something*. In "The Crow," Hoban offers the image of a swaggering crow stealing "leaves of blue heaven under each wing," and in "One Star Less," the poet describes a silent, fallen kite which blots out a star. He writes of "the hem of evening" rustling as she "walks beside the pond." A clever play on words appears in "Typo" which is about the juxtaposition of letters typed on a typewriter keyboard and includes a discussion of the word *nitgub*.

A charming poetry book which enhances an interest in foreign languages as well as in beautiful sounds in English is *A Tune Beyond Us*, a collection of poetry edited by Myra Cohn Livingston, (Harcourt, Brace & World). The poems in this collection range in time from eighth century China to the present. The verses written in other languages appear in both the original and in English translations. For instance, "Winter Song" by Juan Ramón Jiménez has been translated into English by H. R. Hays, but it also appears as "Canción de Invierno." "The Prayer of the Butterfly" by Carmen Bernos de Gasztold has been translated by Rumer Godden, and it also appears as "Prière du Papillon." Poems in this volume offer a beauty of language which is not commonly found in many poetry books designed for children.

Several other poets are interested in creating verses which imaginatively capture an interest in word miracles. Two books by Mary O'Neill are directly related to the wonderland of words. These are

Words, Words, Words (Doubleday & Co.) and *Take a Number* (Doubleday & Co.). In the first, *Words, Words, Words,* the author cleverly gives novel word lore. She directs attention to the fact that no one really knows what the first spoken words were. She writes about the alphabet, Egyptian hieroglyphic writings, early English beginnings, and the written word. Poems about interjections, verbs, nouns, and conjunctions present grammatical concepts rhythmically. Antonyms, synonyms, and homonyms are described in a poem by that title, and different verses describe functions of punctuation marks. These enjoyable background poems are followed by other verses whose lines offer feelings about words. A poem entitled "Hope" offers a vision of grasping for higher goals, and in "Precision" is given a strong sense of the significance of measurement, exactness, and size. This book offers surprise and delight in an original manner to word explorations.

The second book, *Take A Number,* is principally about mathematics, but these verses offer the story of numbers in a colorful, vibrant style. The volume commences with a poem that tells about primitive man counting his animals with pebbles dropped into a bowl, one for each sheep, yak, or foal. The number "one," with its unique qualities, is pursued, and then this idea continues through descriptions of the functions of many other numbers. The poet next transports readers to the world of surprising sets where even vegetable soup is a set, with its vegetables, flavorings, and spices skimming and floating together. Poems about space, time, and other concepts are developed, and one becomes curious about the condition of an imaginary world without mathematics.

Another writer, Eve Merriam, offers numerous versatile poems. Her book, *It Doesn't Always Have to Rhyme* (Atheneum Publishers), makes poetry sparkling fun, and it could also lead to further word explorations by children who are curious to explore word wonderlands. "A Spell of Weather" briefly introduces many terms depicting weather phenomena, from cloudbursts to clearing cerulean blue skies. In "Double Trouble," the poet refreshingly describes scissors and trousers in which two parts are perpetually together. "Mr. Zoo" tells about a composite man who has characteristics acquired from all sorts of animals, and about his wife who also has some zoo traits. A fresh image of a new day is offered in "Metaphor," where the similarity between a willow and a ginkgo is effectively and clearly shown. Modern limericks are given in "Leaning on a Limerick," and onomatopoeia is depicted forcefully through the use of sputtering, splashing words. The writer humorously shatters some time-worn phrases and similes in "A Cliché," and she opens eyes to fresher expressions in an expanding world of the imagination.

A number of experiences with some of these books, activities which may enhance both vocabulary development and creative thinking, follow.

Enrichment Ideas Related to Word Wonderland

THE LEWIS CARROLL CLASSICS

Language Development Activities Related to the Alice Classics

Odd Usages: Pupils can read Chapter 7, "The Mad Tea Party," in *Alice in Wonderland* and compile a list of odd usages of the English language, such as " 'you mean you can't take *less*,' said the Hatter. 'It's very easy to take *more* than nothing.' " (Washington Square Press Edition, p. 65.)

Wonderland Dialogue: The Mock Turtle's curriculum can be studied. This is described in Chapter 9, "The Mock Turtle's Story." Develop a brief bit of conversation between two other animals. One animal can explain his curriculum or course of study.

Jabberwocky Language: In Chapter 17 of *Through the Looking-Glass,* Humpty Dumpty and Alice converse about the meaning of words in the poem, "Jabberwocky," which appears in Chapter 1, "Looking-Glass House." An English book which teaches the structure of our language can be reviewed. Chapters in the Carroll classic can be read, and parts of speech and nonsense words may be listed. Nouns, verbs, and adjectives will be determined according to certain linguistic cues. Some words from this poem may be selected, and Humpty Dumpty's theory of two meanings packed into one word like a portmanteau can be explained.

Clever Puns: A pun consists of the humorous use of two words having the same, or similar, sounds but different meanings; or sometimes, a pun consists of two different or incongruous meanings of the same word. Pupils can work in pairs or in triplets to collect examples of puns in either *Alice in Wonderland* or *Through the Looking-Glass.* Several puns appear in Chapter 9, "Queen Alice," for example, when Alice tells the Red Queen to take some *flour* and the Red Queen wants to know where to pick the *flower.*

Imaginary Letters: Alice can write a letter to Humpty Dumpty thanking him for explaining meanings of words in "Jabberwocky," or the White Rabbit may write a letter to the Duchess apologizing for being late. The Cheshire-Cat could correspond with the Gryphon or the Mock Turtle.

Research Project on Chess: Students may do a research project on the game of chess and compose a two- or three-paragraph essay, "Chess as Seen in Looking-Glass Land."

Study of Tenniel Illustrations: A study of the artist, John Tenniel, who illustrated *Alice's Adventures in Wonderland* published in 1866, and the *Through the Looking-Glass* edition issued in 1872, can be made. *Illustrators of Children's Books 1744-1945,* compiled by Bertha E. Mahony, Louise P. Latimer, and Beulah Folmsbee, (Horn Book), has some details about the relationships between Dodgson and Tenniel. It has been said that Dodgson originally had a thirteenth chapter in *Through the Looking-Glass* which was an incident with a wasp in a wig, but Tenniel persuaded him to eliminate the episode. The class can co-operate in creating a thirteenth chapter to *Through the Looking-Glass.* For instance, a character who has a wasp in his wig may be involved in more nonsensical adventures.

Dramatic Activities Related to the Lewis Carroll Classics

Easy Puppets: Paper spoon or cup puppets, or tongue depresser figures, can be used to reenact "The Walrus and the Carpenter."

Personification: Personification is the giving of life-like qualities to inanimate objects. In the chapter "The Garden of Live Flowers," various flowers talk to each other and to Alice. If possible, live flowers could be collected. Children can form partners and create imaginary conversation while a third pupil serves as the recorder. On the following day, flower puppets can be made of papier-mâché figures or of wooden tongue depressors or spoons and crepe paper. Original puppet plays using personified flower puppets can be created.

Using Tape Recorders and Opaque Projectors: One class used photographs of pupils reading selections from *The Alice in Wonderland* classic. Each photograph was mounted on a sheet decorated with flower petals and the sheet was projected with an opaque projector. The children's voices were taped on a tape recorder. As the audience listened to a particular taped selection, an arrow pointed to the petaled picture of the child reading it.

Mock Television Show: A mock television show can be presented with realia to illustrate a scene from *Through the Looking-Glass.* A frame to represent the looking-glass can be made of wood or cardboard and covered with aluminum foil, silver crepe paper, or paper sprayed with silver paint. Characters in the television skit can walk through the looking-glass frame into Looking-Glass Land.

Composing Additional Episodes: Pupils can imagine that the White Rabbit visits Tweedledum and Tweedledee and can create a dramatization of the Rabbit's encounter with these two characters. The pupils can write the narrative and the dialogue.

Tweedledum and Tweedledee Talk: Pupils may pretend that Tweedledum is a character who has never been to school to learn standard language usage, and that Tweedledee is an educated English scholar who speaks in standard or literary dialect. A dialogue can be de-

Realia for Alice in Wonderland Television
Program — Presented by Jill Maddux, Carol Brenry, Sonja Norman, Sally
Damson, Laura Halpern, and Mary Lou Strack.
Cal-State College,
Hayward, California

veloped and tape-recorded. Tweedledum may be the figure who always
represents poor use of English. A bulletin board of standard and non-
standard English can be arranged, with figures of Tweedledum and
Tweedledee perched at the top of English charts which contrast standard and non-standard classroom talk.

Art and Music Activities Related to the Alice Classics

Pictorial Maps: A board or a table can be used to construct Wonderland, and a three-dimensional map can be made. Bits of sponge or
other material may represent bushes and trees. Various portions of the
map, such as the Tree Home of the Cheshire-Cat or The Queen's Croquet
Ground, should be labeled. A pictorial three-dimensional map of Looking-Glass Land may also be made.

Musical Listening Experiences: One recording, "Alice's Adventures
in Wonderland," has been read and sung by Cyril Ritchard (Riverside

SDP 22). The original music score by Alec Wilder is played by the New York Woodwind Quartet. The carton which contains the records has a facsimile copy of the 1856 edition of *Alice's Adventures in Wonderland* with forty-two illustrations by John Tenniel. Pupils may wish to listen to the recordings of this tale during several sessions.

Song Parodies: Carroll made parodies of songs popular at this time, "Star of the Evening" became the Mock Turtle's "Soup of the Evening," and "Will You Walk into My Parlour?" was parodied as "The Lobster Quadrille." Several current popular songs may be parodied in a nonsensical manner. It might be fun to use some characters from *Through the Looking-Glass,* such as Tweedledum and Tweedledee, and compose a song for them.

Illustrating a Poem by Carroll: Committees can make careful studies of illustrations of *Alice in Wonderland* and *Through the Looking-Glass* which were drawn by Sir John Tenniel. The Washington Square Press edition includes these two classics and a narrative poem, "The Hunting of the Snark." This poem is not illustrated. Pupils may divide responsibilities and draw pictures of characters such as the Bellman, the Beaver, the Snark, Barrister, Boat Maker, and others. Some rare creatures are the Bandersnatch, the Jujub, and the Snark. A roller movie or scroll play based on episodes of the poem can be developed. A tape recorder can add sound effects and some music as background. For instance, bits of music depicting a villain can be played when the Bandersnatch or Jujub appear, or their arrival may be announced by

Alice in Wonderland Figures
Tweedledee and Tweedledum
Television Play
Cal-State College,
Hayward, California

the clanging of cymbals. Portions of the poem may be tape-recorded, and the tape can be played for other classrooms.

A Scrap Materials Box with bits of old mops, colored yarn, buttons, and old cloth such as velvet, silk, or cotton can be brought to the room. Children can use ingenuity in creating such creatures as Snarks, Jujubs, and Bandersnatches and having labels printed on them.

Other Activities Related to "Alice in Wonderland" and "Through the Looking-Glass"

Comparing Editions of the Alice Classic: Several editions of *Alice in Wonderland* may be compared. Three of these are: *Alice's Adventures Underground*, A Facsimile of the Original Lewis Carroll Manuscript (Xerox University of Microfilms Library; *Alice's Adventures through the Looking-Glass and What Alice Found There* (Charles E. Tuttle Co.); and *Alice's Adventures in Wonderland* by Lewis Carroll (Franklin Watts).

Use of Multisensory Aids: A class committee may use many types of multisensory aids to present parts of the Carroll classic. For instance, scenes can be shown on a film strip projector, recordings can be played, and a White Rabbit toy can come to life and speak to listeners.

Mystical Beasts and Monsters

Bandersnatch Episodes: In Chapter 7, "The Lion and the Unicorn," the King says "You might as well try to stop a Bandersnatch." A picture of a lion, a unicorn, and a Bandersnatch can be drawn, and an episode may be added to this chapter depicting Alice's further adventures with a Bandersnatch.

A Bestiary Book: An unusual volume on odd animals is *The Bestiary, A Book of Beasts*, made and edited by T. H. White, (Capricorn Books, G. P. Putnam's Sons). Pupils may find here some beasts which might be added to *Alice in Wonderland* in order to create further episodes which may be illustrated.

Creators of Never, Never Beasts: A book for children on beasts is *The Beasts of Never*, a History of Natural and Unnatural Monsters, Mythical and Magical by Georgess McHargue (Bobbs-Merrill Co.). Another book of this type is *The Most Wonderful Animals that Never Were* by Joseph Wood Krutch (Houghton Mifflin Co.). A third book of unusual beasts is *Not Here and Never Was*, written and illustrated by Virginia Smith, (Harvey House). Richard Armour has also written a clever book, *Odd Old Mammals*, Animals after the Dinosaurs (McGraw-Hill Book Co.). Pupils can create some Never Never Land beasts and develop conversation between them. The beasts can converse with each other, or a modern Alice can visit them.

Papier-Mâché Masks: The Caldecott Award winning picture book, *Where the Wild Things Are,* by Maurice Sendak (Harper & Row) can be read by the pupils. Some masks may be created by using a simple technique with papier-mâché. Heavy tag board may be the base. This can be tied to a plastic chlorinated product container or to a plastic bucket. Parts of egg cartons or other scrap materials may be used for features. A fast method is to dip larger sheets of paper in wallpaper paste and wrap them around a mask base. Pupils who wish to make their masks more artistic may use narrow strips of paper dipped in paste and attach them to the mask foundation. If children are to talk with the mask on, several holes will have to be made for the sound to come out. Otherwise, conversation should be recorded on a tape. The children can pantomime events while the tape is being played.

Creating Poetry on Bumptious Beasts: Another book for younger children is the *A.B.C. of Bumptious Beasts* by Gail Kredenser and Stanley Mosk (Harlan Quist Books, Crown Publishers). Boys and girls may read these poems, and a first or second grade class can create a *Bumptious Beast Book.* Pictures of beasts can be painted, and pairs of children can work on couplets or quatrains to complete poetic stories to match the pictures.

Paper Zoo Composite Animals: Boys and girls may listen to reading from *A Paper Zoo,* a Collection of Animal Poems by Modern American Poets, edited by Renée Weiss, (Macmillan Co.). This volume does not include nonsense animals, but does have pictures of the sloth, the jellyfish, and others. Pupils can use simple reference books containing many pictures to find other odd-looking animals, or they can create a nonsense animal by taking parts of two animals and joining them together to make a new one.

Creating Parodies of Animal Poetry: A book for older pupils, compiled by Gwendolyn Reed, is *Out of the Ark* (Atheneum Publishers). It includes poems such as "Take Any Bird" by Geoffrey Chaucer, and one written by Frances Jammes and translated from the French by Richard Wilbur, "A Prayer to Go to Paradise with the Donkey." Pupils can read these poems and create parodies of them.

Activities Related to "The Hunting of the Snark"

Writing Quatrains: "The Hunting of the Snark" is a narrative verse written in rhythmical quatrains. Lines one and three rhyme, as do lines two and four. After the pupils have read the whole poem several times, they may omit the last two quatrains of "The Vanishing" section and create new ones.

Extension of the Poem: The narrative theme can be extended by adding several additional quatrains. Characters of a Boojum and a Bandersnatch may be expanded, and poster paints or watercolors can be used to decorate them.

A Sheriff's "WANTED" Handbill: A character, such as the Boojum or the Bandersnatch, can be chosen, and a "WANTED" poster, similar to sheriffs' handbills in pioneer Western towns, can be created.

ACTIVITIES RELATED TO EDWARD LEAR

Study of the Limerick Form: Pupils can study the typical limerick pattern. They will note that the limerick is a five-line verse in *The Book of Nonsense,* edited by R. L. Green, (E. P. Dutton & Co.), but that it has a four-line stanza form in *The Complete Nonsense Book* by Edward Lear which was edited by Lady Strachey (Dodd, Mead & Co.). A typical limerick written by a child and included in Ruth Kearney Carlson's *Language Sparklers for the Intermediate Grades* (Wagner Printing Co.) is:

BLOND HAIR
There once was a girl with blond hair
Who one day was chased by a bear
　　She ran up a tree
　　But she couldn't see
Why the bear didn't care for blond hair.

A limerick rhyme pattern is:

1	....	a
2	....	a
3	....	b
4	....	b
5	....	a

All lines with the letter "a" (lines 1, 2, 5) rhyme with each other. Lines 3 and 4 rhyme. Sometimes the last line repeats several words appearing on the first line. This means less rhyming for children.

Creating Original Limericks: Edward Lear was first of all an artist; later he became a nonsense poet. Pupils can create caricatures of human beings, drawings which reveal ludicrous characteristics such as big ears, flat feet, extended necks, or luminous noses. They can observe how Dr. Seuss (Theodore Geisel) made odd sketches of animals and people. After a ridiculous figure has been drawn, pupils can create an original limerick to accompany the illustration.

Comparing Art Illustrations: The illustrations in *Limericks by Lear,* with verses by Edward Lear and pictures by Lois Ehlert, (World Pub-

lishing Co.) may be contrasted with pictures drawn by Lear to illustrate his "Eight-and-Forty Nonsense Limericks," edited by R. L. Green
and published in *The Book of Nonsense*, (E. P. Dutton & Co.).

Making Flannelgraph Pictures and Figures: In 1968, Harper &
Row published *The Scroobious Pip* which was for the most part, written
by Edward Lear. It was later completed by Ogden Nash and beautifully illustrated by Nancy Ekholm Burkert. In this poem, all of the
animals of the world gather around a strange creature which is part
bird, part beast, part man, part insect, and part fish, and which bears
the name of the Scroobious Pip. After the poem is read to the children,
but without showing Nancy Burkert's illustrations, they can make
flannelgraph figures or pictures that develop the characteristics of the
Scroobious Pip as the poem progresses. When the pupils have had
time to create their imaginative images of this unusual creature, the
work of the professional artist can be shown to them.

Ogden Nash Inserts: In the Burkert edition, brackets are used to
indicate words or phrases omitted by Lear from the poem. Pupils can
pretend that they are Ogden Nash and supply the special words or
terms for the missing portions of the original Lear poem.

Dioramas or Peep Shows: A popular nonsense poem by Lear is
"The Jumblies." This appears separately as a book, *The Jumblies*, which
has been illustrated by Edward Gorey, (William R. Scott). Pupils can
make a diorama or peep box in which scenes from "The Jumblies" can
be reenacted.

Personifying Inanimate Objects: In the poem, "The Nutcrackers
and the Sugar-Tongs," Lear illustrates several examples of personification. The Sugar-Tongs and the Nutcrackers converse. The Frying-Pan
speaks, and the Tea-Kettle hisses. Pupils can collect objects from magazine advertisements and use them on a flannelgraph board. Dialogue
between these inanimate objects can be created. For instance, a silver
spoon can converse with a rocking chair, or a television set may talk
to a rug. Later, these personified objects can be "written in" to a
poem or a story. Another one of Lear's poems of this type is "The
Broom, the Shovel, the Poker, and the Tongs."

Unusual Milliners: An unusual hat appears in Lear's poem, "The
Quangle-Wangle's Hat." Boys and girls can read or listen to this poem
and then create their own Quangle-Wangle Hats after which a Style
Show can be held.

Nonsense Day Book Sharing: A Nonsense Day Fair can be held.
Children may bring some nonsense books to class or select humorous
poems or stories from books and share a bit of nonsense with others.

Some books which they may wish to obtain are the following:

CARROLL, LEWIS. *Jabberwocky and Other Frabjous Nonsense.* Pictures by Simms Taback. New York: A Harlan Quist Book. Distributed by Crown Publishers, 1967.

GROSS, SARAH CHOKLA. *Every Child's Book of Verse.* Illustrated by Martha Cone. New York: Franklin Watts, 1968.

LEAR, EDWARD. *The Jumblies.* Drawings by Edward Gorey. New York: William R. Scott, 1968.

Lear's Nonsense Verses. Pictures by Tomi Ungerer. New York: Grosset & Dunlap, 1967.

LEAR, EDWARD. *Two Laughable Lyrics.* "The Pobble Who Has No Toes" and "The Quangle Wangle's Hat." Illustrated by Paul Galdone. New York: G. P. Putnam's Sons, 1968.

———. *Nonsense Book.* Boston: Little, Brown & Co., 1888.

The twenty-sixth printing has been made of this book which has all of the original illustrations.

———. *First Publication of This Lear Alphabet ABC.* New York: McGraw-Hill Book Co., 1965.

This book, which is in cursive writing, was penned and illustrated by Edward Lear.

———. *The Four Little Children Who Went Around the World.* Pictures by Arnold Lobel. New York: Macmillan Co., 1968.

A nonsense tale concerning four children who sailed around the world visiting curious lands and seeing odd creatures, such as Bluebottle Flies, Crabbees, and the Cooperative Cauliflower.

PRELUTSKY, JACK, trans. *No End of Nonsense.* Translated from the German. Pictures by Wilfred Blecher. New York: Macmillan Co., 1968.

This is a refreshingly original nonsense book in which one sees oxen upside down, gnats and flies in identical size, and an "Upside Down and Inside Out Farm."

SMITH, WILLIAM JAY. *Mr. Smith and Other Nonsense.* Illustrated by Don Bolognese. New York: Delacorte Press, 1968.

Here is another author who collects nonsensical ideas. This volume includes poems of sense and nonsense, as well as an interesting collection of limericks and verses about birds, beasts, and unusual people. Most of the verse is in the tradition of Lewis Carroll and Edward Lear.

The Walloping Window Blind. Illustrated by Harry Devlin. Princeton, N. J.: D. Van Nostrand Co., 1968.

WITHERS, CARL. *The World of Nonsense.* Illustrated by John E. Johnson. Holt, Rinehart & Winston, 1968.

Includes strange and humorous tales from many lands.

ACTIVITIES RELATED TO "THE WONDERFUL O" AND
"THE NIGHT THEY STOLE THE ALPHABET"

Creating an Alphabet Tale: An original tale in the Thurber style, similar to his *The Wonderful O,* may be created. Pupils can select another vowel, such as *E* or *A,* and develop a story showing what might happen if one of these letters would be banished from a kingdom or a country.

An Alphabet Court Trial: Pupils may develop an imaginary court scene in which a prisoner is brought to trial for an offense such as swallowing all the E's in the country. Principals in the dramatization could be the judge, the jury members, the defendant, the prosecuting and defending attornies, witnesses, the bailiff, the clerk, and a policeman.

A Stolen Alphabet Game: Children can imagine that the whole alphabet has been stolen, and a game can be created in which alphabetical letters are hidden in various odd places.

Newspaper Features and Want Ads: Pupils can write an imaginary news article according to the journalistic style of a daily newspaper. The article should include a headline and details concerning stolen alphabet letters. Or they can write items for the classified advertising section of a newspaper. These items can be aptly worded requests for the return of stolen alphabet letters.

ACTIVITIES BASED ON "THE PHANTOM TOLLBOOTH"

Dictionopolis: Activities in Dictionopolis described in the April, 1964 issue of *Elementary English* are sufficient to last from four to six months if children become this much interested in the miracle of words.

Word Cart: A miniature cart can be made with a "For Sale" sign on it. Unusual words can be placed in the cart, and peddlers can buy and sell words. In some cases, barter will be used; in other instances, a word will be so valuable that additional money will be needed.

A Word Court Trial: An imaginary court trial can be held and words can be put on trial for the damage that they have done to the world. Words such as treason, escalation, cold war, missiles, atom bombs, could be used.

"Silence is Golden" Pantomimes: Children can pantomime sentences or stories while a stage manager displays the sign, "Silence is Golden."

Murals and Friezes: Committees can be encouraged to make murals or friezes. Such sites as the Sea of Knowledge, the Kingdom of Wisdom, the Mountains of Ignorance, Digitopolis—the City of Numbers, can be depicted.

Miniature Toys: Miniature dolls can be dressed as Princesses of Rhyme and Reason, and rhymes or songs may be composed for the princesses to recite.

Word Banquet: A royal banquet can be held for Kings and Queens. At the banquet, stunts can be performed as, for instance, a cliché such as "Have a Square Meal" could be portrayed with imaginary food items on the menu arranged in squares.

Imaginative Mail Boxes: Decorate attractive mail boxes by covering containers with gift paper and printing such titles as:

Words I Know
Words I Never Need
Words I Need Constantly
Words which Bring Beauty and Happiness

Pupils can think of words which are appropriate and then mail them in the proper mail box. At the end of a period of time, these words may be compiled into categories and word lists.

OTHER ACTIVITIES RELATED TO THE MIRACLE OF WORDS

The following series of activities may be developed in connection with the reading of any book or of several books connected with the Wonderland of Words.

"Lovely Words" Chart: A list of words which seem beautiful or lovely to members of the class can be compiled and placed on an attractive chart with illustrations.

Onomatopoetic Word Story with Sound Effects: Onomatopoeia and onomatopoetic words can be discussed. An original story can be created, and rhythm instruments may be used to supply sound effects. Onomatopoetic words which sound like their meaning (such as *squishy* and *squashy*) should be used in the story.

Colorful Homonym Trees: A branch from a real tree could be used for a homonym tree. It can be sprayed and colored gold or silver. Homonyms may be printed on colorful cardboard butterflies, birds, or fruit, and then hung on the tree.

Homonym Talk Fest: The children can hold talking periods during which they use homonyms in sentences. This can be done as a

Felt Board—Flannel Graph Figure
Melinda Lo Savio
Cal State College,
Hayward, California

contest, with scores being given for the correct use of homonyms in sentences.

Homonym Treasure Hunts: Have homonym treasure hunts. Winners are the pupils who present the longest list of homonyms. It is important to encourage pupils to use homonyms in context.

Writing an Original Foreign Language Book: If a foreign language is being studied, a simple book which is bilingual in nature can be designed for very young children. It should have pictures, as well as words and phrases in English, and corresponding words and phrases in the foreign language.

ACTIVITIES RELATED TO POETRY

Language Activities Related to Poetry Books

Making a Word Book: Several modern poetry books include numerous poems related to language activities. One section in *An Invitation to Poetry,* selected by Marjory Lawrence, (Addison-Wesley Publishing Co.) is "Conversations in Another Language." Included here are poems such as "Conversation" by Eve Merriam; "La Cucaracha," "Mis Tres Amigos," and "Madame Sans-Souci" by Lillian Bragdon, as well as many others. These poems can be read and differences in idiomatic language phrases may be compared. Another section in this same volume entitled "The Way of Words" includes poems such as "Nym and Graph" by Eve Merriam; "Put an I before E," "Why I Did Not Reign," and "A Teacher Whose Spelling's Unique" by Charles B. Loomis; and "Spelling Bee" by David McCord. These have interesting lines about words and peculiar spellings. Pupils may like to start a collection of other poems about language or spelling and make a Word Book.

Couplet Countdowns and Count-Ups: *An Invitation to Poetry* includes "Couplet Countdown" by Eve Merriam. Pupils can create a Couplet Countdown in which the number of words becomes less and less; or a Couplet Count-Up in which each couplet may expand the number of words to a line.

Writing Original Limericks: *A Beginning Book of Poems,* with poems selected by Marjory Lawrence, (Addison-Wesley Publishing Co.) has two poems about limericks. They are "The Limerick's Lively to Write" and "Write a Limerick Now," by David McCord. Some limericks by Edward Lear may be reread, as well as some by other modern humorists. Pupils can write and illustrate original limericks.

Fresh Imagery for Clichés: After reading "A Cliché" by Eve Merriam, pupils can gather clichés from conversation and literature. Original similes or metaphors may be created as substitutes for worn-out phrases.

Occupational Jargon: One subject or occupation can be selected and a poem about it written in couplets or quatrains using correct professional terminology in a manner similar to that used in the poem, "A Spell of Weather," by Eve Merriam. The lawyer, the carpenter, the baseball player, the musician, and the doctor each uses words and phrases which are appropriate to his particular occupation. Attention should be focused upon one vocation or hobby, and ideas can be expressed around a central theme. Words which give significant clues to the job or profession should be used.

Poetry Activities Using Color

Poems and Stories about Color: In a section, "Colors Dance and Colors Sing" appearing in *A Beginning Book of Poems,* certain poems included are related to color. One of these is "The Colors" by Mary O'Neill. Another is "Paint" by Ilo Orleans. Pupils may collect other poems about colors, such as "Silver" by Walter de la Mare, and poems appearing in *Hailstones and Halibut Bones* by Mary O'Neill (Doubleday & Co.). Other imaginative books about color include *Red Is Never a Mouse* by Clifford Eth (Bobbs-Merrill Co.); *Creating Clear Images* by Margaret Fisher Hertel, Marion H. Smith, and Betty O'Connor (Fidelier Co.), *Tico and the Golden Wings* by Leo Lionni (Pantheon Books), and *What Is Color?* by Alice and Martin Provensen (Golden Press). Several color activities can be developed from these volumes.

Word Scene Bulletin Boards and Friezes: The teacher and class should together read fresh, modern poetry which is not stereotyped in nature. Good, clear poetic images can be shared, and an interest center may be created to display beautiful phrases, similes, metaphors, and images. For instance, a lovely picture of an Ice Palace may be painted in blues, greens, purples, and white, with glitter to add glamor. Poems and stories about the cold northland or other icy areas can be read, and effective word pictures can be attached to the ice palace scene.

Another mural or frieze might be one of beautiful lakes or the trickling sound of waterfalls and fountains, with appropriate words to go with sparkling waters.

A third one might be a colorful Mexican market scene, with dashes of brilliant color. Mexican words or phrases can be printed either underneath or on strips of paper attached to the mural.

A fourth idea is an Outer Space mural which can serve as the background for newly coined space terminology.

Establishing Color Centers of Interest: A special center of interest can be created. For instance, one featuring purple could have an arrangement including a purple scarf, purple grapes, and a ceramic purple cow. Pupils could find a suitable place in this setting for a poem about the color purple.

Extending Color Vocabularies: Pupils can arrange color rainbows to include twelve to fifteen variations of any one color. For instance, such a rainbow can be made with fourteen blues, among them, marine blue, navy blue, robin's egg blue, turquoise, and others.

Finger Painting Color Scenes: Younger children may finger paint a scene and name it as if it were an artist's masterpiece such as "Studies in Peppermint Pink" or "A Blue-Studded Sky."

Making Silhouettes: Dark silhouette figures can be arranged against a brilliantly painted background as for instance, a sunburst scene.

Creating Original Color Verses: Pupils may compose free verse or rhymes which focus upon one color, as Mary O'Neill does in *Hailstones and Halibut Bones,* (Doubleday & Co.).

Using Color Tone Poems: Visual and auditory imagery can be synchronized by using a recording such as "Frank Sinatra Conducts Tone Poems in Color," Capitol Records, T 735. Some sample lessons with children's poetry relating to color appear in *Poetry for Today's Child* by Ruth Kearney Carlson, (F. A. Owen Publishers).

Writing a Parody of "Red Is Never a Mouse": After enjoying *Red Is Never a Mouse,* children can create a cooperative class story in a similar way by writing a book such as *Green Is Never a Dog* or *White Is Never a Lion.* After an idea has been used, they may draw colorful illustrations to accompany the script.

Creating a Flannelgraph Story on "Tico and the Golden Wings": Flannelgraph figures can be created to go with this book. Children can tell the story and let other classmates add colored feathers to Tico.

"Stories about Colors" (*Coronet*): Six filmstrips and recordings of *Stories about Colors* are distributed by Coronet. These include: The Purple Flower, The Orange Pumpkin, The Yellow Bird, The Green Caterpillar, The Blue Balloon, and The Red Car. After viewing these filmstrips and listening to the Sound Version S134, episodes for *A Color Story* can be created. A cooperative story can be told in a kindergarten or a first grade class.

Poetry on the Wishing Theme

Wishing-Bird Wishes: In *Tico and the Golden Wings* by Leo Lionni, a Wishing-Bird grants wishes. One child may be chosen as a Wishing-Bird, and other boys and girls can write or draw pictures of wishes on a colorful piece of paper. The Wishing-Bird can collect the wishes and attach them to a colorful Wishing-Tree.

Aladdin's Magic Lamp: Annette Wynne's "I Keep Three Wishes Ready," from *The First Book of Poetry,* selected by Isabel Peterson, (Franklin Watts), can be read, and Aladdin's magic lamp can be displayed. A watering can or a silver gravy boat resemble the fairy tale lamp. Children can be encouraged to tiptoe up to the teacher, rub the lamp three times, and whisper a wish into her ear. After this, they can return to their places to paint pictures of their favorite wishes. They can form sharing groups to discuss their wishes.

Reality and Fantasy Language Thinking Charts: In *Sam Bangs and Moonshine,* written and illustrated by Evaline Ness, (Holt, Rinehart & Winston), Samantha discusses real things and fanciful things. Two columnar charts can be made. At the top of one, pictures of fairies, elves, leprechauns, and goblins can appear. At the top of the other chart, pictures of food, clothing, homes, and occupations can be attached. Pupils can supply lists of real things which can be placed under the real column and fanciful things which can appear under the fanciful column.

Miscellaneous Poetry Activities

Dancing Poetry: A collection titled "Rhymes and Rhythms" appears in *Poems and Verses to Begin On,* edited by Donald J. Bissett, (Chandler Publishing Co.). This collection includes the verses, "Jump or Jiggle" by Evelyn Beyer; "The Pickety Fence" and "Song of the Train" by David McCord; and "Trains" by James S. Tippett. The class can be divided into subgroups. One group can chant the verse in choral verse style while the other enacts the poems through creative rhythms and dance. *Learning through Movement* by Betty Rowen (Teachers College Press) has numerous suggestions on ways to correlate creative movement with literature.

Animal Poetry: A second book of poetry and verse for urban children, edited by Donald J. Bissett, is *Poems and Verses about Animals* (Chandler Publishing Co.). An Animal Zoo can be made for the room. Three-dimensional figures can be created through the use of corrugated cardboard, egg cartons, and scrap materials. Pupils can chant animal poems while other children manipulate corresponding animal puppets made of simple sticks, cardboard, socks, or paper bags. An animal vocabulary book showing pictures and names for animals can be developed. In some of the poems in Bissett's book, words like goose and gosling, hen and chicken, have been used to differentiate between adult and young animals.

Photography and Poetry: Children can make a collection of black and white photographs taken of city scenes. These photos can accompany various poems describing urban scenes such as "Subway Rush Hour," or "Harlem Night Song," by Langston Hughes; or "The Flower-Cart Man," and "Manhattan Lullaby," by Rachel Field. These poems appear in the volume, *On City Streets*, an Anthology of Poetry Selected by Nancy Larrick, (M. Evans & Co.).

Professor Swigly Brown's Poetry: In *Take Sky*, More Rhymes of the Never Was and Always Is, (Little, Brown & Co.) David McCord, has Professor Swigly Brown expound on the couplet, the quatrain, the limerick, and the triolet. The professor cleverly describes these poetic forms. After studying these structures carefully, children can create some original couplets, quatrains, limericks, and triolets.

Conclusion

Words can sparkle and spin, or whistle and whine, and children should have numerous experiences in tuning their ears in to the glory and mystery of a Wonderland of Words. The next chapter will treat of ways in which Oriental artists have expanded words and syllables into sparse, beautiful poetic verse patterns.

SELECTED REFERENCES FOR CHILDREN

ARMOUR, RICHARD. *Odd Old Mammals*, Animals after the Dinosaurs. Illustrated by Paul Galdone. New York: McGraw-Hill Book Co., 1968.

BISSETT, DONALD J., ed. *Poems and Verses to Begin On*. San Francisco: Chandler Publishing Co., 1967.

————. ed. *Poems and Verses about Animals*. San Francisco: Chandler Publishing Co., 1967.

CARROLL, LEWIS. *Jabberwocky and Other Frabjous Nonsense*. Pictures by Simms Taback. New York: A Harlin Quist Book. Distributed by Crown Publishers, 1967.

————. *Alice in Wonderland and Other Favorites*. Illustrated by John Tenniel. New York: Washington Square Press, 1960 printing.

————. *Alice's Adventure Underground*, A Facsimile of the Original Lewis Carroll Manuscript. Ann Arbor: Xerox University Microfilm Library, 1964.

————. *Alice's Adventures through the Looking-Glass and What Alice Found There*. Illustrated by Peter Newell. Rutland, N. J.: Charles E. Tuttle Co., 1968.

————. *Alice's Adventures in Wonderland*. Illustrated by Arthur Rackham. New York: Franklin Watts. Reprinted 1966.

COLE, WILLIAM, comp. *Oh, What Nonsense!* Illustrated by Tomi Ungerer. New York: The Viking Press, 1966.

————. *Frances Face-Maker*: A Going to Bed Book. Illustrated by Tomi Ungerer. Cleveland: World Publishing Co., 1963.

————, comp. *Beastly Boys and Ghastly Girls*. Illustrated by Tomi Ungerer. Cleveland: World Publishing Co., 1964.

EPSTEIN, SAM and BERYL. *The First Book of Words,* Their Family History. Illustrated by Laszlo Roth. New York: Franklin Watts, 1954.

ETH, CLIFFORD. *Red Is Never a Mouse.* Illustrated by Bill Hecker. Indianapolis: The Bobbs-Merrill Co., 1960.

ETS, MARIE HALL. *Talking without Words.* New York: The Viking Press, 1968.

GRAHAM, JOHN. *A Crowd of Cows.* Illustrations by Feodor Rojankovsky. New York: Harcourt, Brace & World, 1968.

GREEN, R. L., ed. *The Book of Nonsense.* New York: E. P. Dutton & Co., 1956.

GREET, W. CABELL; JENKINS, WILLIAM A.; and SCHILLER, ANDREW. *In Other Words,* A Beginning Thesaurus. Glenview, Ill.: Scott, Foresman & Co., 1968.

GROSS, SARAH CHOKLA. *Every Child's Book of Verse.* Illustrated by Martha Cone. New York: Franklin Watts, 1968.

HAUTZIG, ESTHER. *At Home: A Visit in Four Languages.* Illustrated by Aliki. New York: Macmillan Co., 1968.

—————. *In the Park.* An Excursion in Four Languages. Illustrated by Ezra Jack Keats. New York: Macmillan Co., 1968.

HOBAN, RUSSELL. *The Pedaling Man and Other Poems.* New York: W. W. Norton & Co., 1968.

JOSLIN, SESYLE. *The Night They Stole the Alphabet.* Illustrated by Enrico Arno. New York: Harcourt, Brace & World, 1968.

JUSTER, NORTON. *The Phantom Tollbooth.* Illustrations by Jules Feiffer. New York: Random House, 1961.

KREDENSER, GAIL, and MOSK, STANLEY. *The ABC of Bumptious Beasts.* Harlin Quist, Crown Publishers, 1966.

KRUTCH, JOSEPH WOOD. *The Most Wonderful Animals that Never Were.* Illustrated by Pauline Baynes. Boston: Houghton Mifflin Co., 1969.

LARRICK, NANCY, selected by. *On City Streets,* An Anthology of Poetry. Photographs by David Sagarin. New York: M. Evans & Co. Distributed by J. B. Lippincott Co., Philadelphia, 1968.

LAWRENCE, MARJORY, selected by. *A Beginning Book of Poems.* Menlo Park, California: Addison-Wesley Publishing Co., 1967.

—————, selected by. *An Invitation to Poetry.* Menlo Park, California: Addison-Wesley Publishing Co., 1967.

LEAR, EDWARD. *The Scroobious Pip.* Completed by Ogden Nash. Illustrated by Nancy Ekholm Burkert. New York: Harper & Row, 1968.

—————. *Two Laughable Lyrics.* "The Pobble Who Has No Toes" and "The Quangle Wangle's Hat." Illustrated by Paul Galdone. New York: G. P. Putnam's Sons, 1966.

—————. *The Jumblies.* Illustrated by Edward Gorey. New York: William R. Scott, 1968.

Lear's Nonsense Verses. Pictures by Tomi Ungerer. New York: Grosset & Dunlap, 1967.

LEAR, EDWARD. *Limericks by Lear.* Illustrated by Lois Ehlert. Cleveland: World Publishing Co., 1965.

—————. *The Complete Nonsense Book.* Edited by Lady Strachey. New York: Dodd, Mead & Co., 1964 printing.

—————. *Nonsense Book.* Boston: Little, Brown & Co., 1888.

—————. Penned and illustrated by. *First Publication of This Lear Alphabet ABC.* New York: McGraw-Hill Book Co., 1965.

chapter 3

dragonflies and frogs

Oriental Types of Poetry and Beauty

In our present mechanized, computerized world, children need a glimpse of the beautiful things in life to contrast with ugly concrete freeways and desolate air-polluted dumps of human waste which they often see. Much of beauty lies in an appreciation of natural phenomena—the disheveled swallow seeking shelter under roof eaves, the willow gracefully bending its limbs near a duck pond, or Bridal Veil Falls tossing dainty sprays of mist in a light breeze. A child who learns to appreciate loveliness improves his power to sensitize and reflect, and he acquires acute observational skills. Sensitivity toward beauty can also come from an enhanced awareness of Oriental literature and art, and many books on Japanese poetry and art are currently being written for children. This chapter will discuss Oriental aesthetics and types of poetry and art.

For more than twelve hundred years, the Japanese people, ranging from titled nobility to lowly peasants, have purposely cultivated an appreciation of beauty known as *shibui*. One object is generally considered to be more lovely than a mass of things. The philosopher-poet speaks of one plum blossom, a branch of a persimmon tree, or the cawing of a lonely ebony crow. Developing an awareness of beauty brings a quiet sense of revelation, but a *shibui* type of beauty has its high C as well as its quiet note. The poet sees a lonely gull silhouetted against a gray sky in the stillness of an autumn evening. He is lonely, and he senses the isolation of the gull also. He experiences darkness and melancholy as he views the gray feathers touching the edges of a leaden sky. One way the Japanese people have of expressing their sensitivity to beauty is in a seventeen-syllable poem, the *haiku*, the

50

popularity of which is marked by the fact that more than 41,000 verses were entered in a Japan Air Lines National Contest in 1964.

The Haiku Verse Form

As translated and published in English, the *haiku* is usually a seventeen-syllable verse form which contains a seasonal word and is arranged in lines of five, seven, and five syllables. It may be rhymed or unrhymed, but most translations usually present it in an unrhymed form. Certain characteristics differentiate it from other poetic genre. First of all, an aware reader of *haiku* feels a closeness to nature, for the poet has not written about a object as if he is observing it from a distance. He speaks of a frog as if he has a sense of identity with it. Nothing is too insignificant for such a verse. A poet sings of a cricket or a grasshopper, of the dry grass or the distant mountain, of the empty rice bowl or the clinging morning glory vine.

In many anthologies of Japanese poetry, verse is organized according to a season. This sensitivity to nature according to seasons is noted in Volume III, *Summer-Autumn* by R. H. Blyth (The Hokuseido Press). Reading these verses, one glimpses a flash of lightning and the screech of a night heron, trickling waters on a leaking roof disturbing a nest of wasps, rain beating down on the heads of carp, a line of ants, a summer moon emerging from a mosquito net, a spotted turtle running along a hill, or a tiny crablet reflected in clear, blue water. A sensitive reader sees the injured bleeding hands of the stonemasons or the glowing elegance of azaleas, and becomes aware of a relatedness between the two. The gifted imaginative eyes of the poet, Buson, glimpse a scarlet peony, a silver cat, and a golden butterfly all interwoven into a meaningful whole. Natural phenomena are encountered in many verses of this type, and the reader can't help but feel this closeness to nature.

A second element of *haiku* is a "suchness" of things. The poet does not write about ugliness and joy per se; he writes about things which he feels deeply. His creative ability comes from his acute awareness of what he senses or feels, and this sensitivity toward his environment is filtered through his being. Some of these verses do not have a full depth of meaning for an American child unless he knows something about their background. For example, in *A History of Haiku*, Volume Two, (The Hokuseido Press), Blyth translates a few poems by Shiki. One short verse on page 91 of this volume speaks of hollyhocks being trampled on the ground at a festival. An American child reading this verse gets an image of cerise or lavender hollyhocks being trampled by indifferent persons. However, the poem has deep significance in Japan where, in the city of Kyoto, a Hollyhock Festival is celebrated annually on the fifteenth of May. On this day, hollyhocks decorate the gates of houses, and people wear the flowers on their clothes and in their hair. The supply of hollyhocks is so abundant that some of them do get trodden, and this is the significance of the hollyhock poem.

Another poem by Shiki speaks of the toll of a bell and the thudding sound of falling, ripe persimmons. Blyth interprets this to mean that the thudding sound of the falling fruit and the tolling of the bell are almost equal in significance. This poem illustrates a third element of *haiku*, the careful selectivity of words.

Japanese poets spend hours poring over word books, diaries, and books of the seasons. This third quality of good *haiku* is the utilization of just the right word to express a particular feeling. Since the poet is limited to compressing his thoughts into a framework of only seventeen syllables, the structural limitations of this form necessitate a careful choice of the precise word to express a desired mood. Therefore, in the Shiki poem about a tolling bell and the sound of falling ripe persimmons, the selection of the word *thudding* is significant because a *thud* is a dull heavy sound or thumping. The bell *tolls*, it does not clang, or peal, or tinkle. When a bell tolls, its sound comes slowly and at regular intervals. The contrast between *thud* and *toll* is such that a feeling of equal power is felt between Shiki's fondness for persimmon fruit and the mysterious call of a temple bell.

The use of a seasonal word is a fourth element of traditional *haiku*. This further adds to the compression, or brevity, of the verse. Japanese poets of the Muromachi period, from 1324 to 1549, depicted a seasonal image in each natural phenomenon of the moon—a cherry blossom or a frog. Anthologists of *haiku* verse usually arrange their compilations according to a seasonal framework, and this is also followed for the *saijiki*, or index of seasonal words. "On Haiku and Haiga: An Essay," appears in *A Net of Fireflies*, Japanese Haiku and Haiku Paintings, with verse translations by Harold Stewart (Charles E. Tuttle Co.). This essay discusses the seasonal reference (*kisetsu*), or the word or phrase which will establish the time of year. Several important *kisetsu* of seasonal words forming themes for *haiku* appear on pages 144 and 145 of this volume.

Kenneth Yasuda discusses the seasonal element in several pages of his scholarly volume, *The Japanese Haiku*, Its Essential Nature, History, and Possibilities in English, with Selected Examples (Charles E. Tuttle Co.). Poems about the spring theme usually include an image of a nightingale, a plum blossom, or a cherry blossom. The cuckoo is the seasonal word for summer in many verses. In 1636, the *Hanabigusa* by Rippo listed approximately 650 seasonal words. The *Haikai Saijiki* of 1803 has 2600 items. Even certain words have delicate nuances. Flowers with young leaves belong to spring, but the word "flowers" itself usually symbolizes summer.

A fifth element of *haiku* is its openness to different ideas and interpretations. The poet suggests an idea, but its full significance is to be completed by the imaginative skill of the reader. In other words, the connoisseur of Japanese poetry becomes an experiencer. A few words are used to offer sharp images and a sketch of a poem, and the reader visually or aurally completes the meaning in his imagination.

This openness to different interpretations in *haiku* is similar to the skilled emptiness found in Japanese brush paintings. In his volume, *The Way of Zen* (Pantheon Books), Alan W. Watts describes this calligraphic style of painting which is created with black ink on paper or on silk. The painting was done with ink which had been formed into a solid stick. The *sumi*, or ink stick, was used during the Chou Period (1122-249 B.C.) in China and was made from a mixture of soot from burned red pine, paulownia,, hempseed, and rapeseed oil. The mixture was blended, molded, and dried in the shade. Some water was poured into a small stone dish and the black ink stick was rubbed in it until the desired blackness was obtained. The brush, or ye-fude, was the end of a bamboo stem, which had a few sharply-pointed bristles. Materials for the brush were animal hair, fur, fibre, rice straw, or feathers. The touch of the brush was light and fluid. This was known as *Sumi-e* painting. It was developed during the Tang dynasty around A.D. 700-760 and artists during the Sung dynasty, A.D. 959-1279, perfected the style. They became landscape painters, and their "nature paintings" showed mountains, mists, trees, rocks, and birds. This type of art is still a popular form of Oriental expression.

Sumi-e painting has an apparent emptiness. The artist fills in one corner or part of a picture, bringing a sense of movement to the whole scene. Form is balanced with emptiness, and the imaginative eye of the viewer must complete the picture much in the same manner that a reader must complete a *haiku* poem. A recent book about this form of art is *Sumi-e* by Chiura Obata (Daiichi Seihan Co.). The volume includes scenes portraying various strokes and showing movements of maple leaves, insects, morning glories, and mountain mists. One senses the significance of nature in the wildness of "Unfinished Symphony," a painting which is reproduced in the Chiura Obata volume.

Children who wish to know more about Japanese art as being a part of the cultural background of Japanese poetry may wish to read Elizabeth Ripley's *Hokusai, a Biography* (J. B. Lippincott Co.). This book, which is about a nineteenth century Japanese artist, contains thirty-two photographs of the artist's work and could conceivably inspire older children to become artists. *The Cat Who Went to Heaven* by Elizabeth Coatsworth, illustrated by Lynd Ward, (Macmillan Co.) is a story that beautifully portrays Oriental art. The masterpiece for the Buddha is the basis for the plot which further shows that much of *haiku* verse and Oriental art are unfinished statements—to be completed by the experiencer.

A sense of *immediacy,* or an involvement in the present, is a sixth quality found in *haiku* verses. One feels an "instantaneous perception or simultaneity" in much Japanese poetry. Past, present, and future hours are fused into one terse verse. This sense of the ever-present now is enjoyed by children who dislike waiting for illusory promises of the future.

In two of his poems appearing in *Cricket Songs,* translated by Harry Behn (Harcourt Brace & World), Basho immerses himself with a lowly frog and the cicadas. In the first poem, he feels the silence of an old pond disturbed by a frog — then there is silence again. In the second poem, Basho senses stillness being disturbed by buzzing cicadas drilling a hole in a rock. An equivalence of feeling and image mark Japanese poetry of the highest quality. It is poor *haiku* if a reader is unable to grasp an image or a picture through the skillful use of words.

Another quality of good Japanese verse is more than mere *imagery.* The image must reenforce the poetic mood of the creator. Most poems depict a single object—a blushing peony, stamens of a white calla lily, a crimson dragonfly, or a lizard slithering along with undulating ripples. These images must be clear, but a sincere feeling of man's relationship to a natural object must accompany them. The poet does not look at a mountain; he becomes a part of the mountain, and the mountain becomes a part of him. Nature is a part of man, and the Oriental poet does not feel antagonistic toward it. A mountain is not to be conquered; it is to be *felt.* In the second volume, *A History of Haiku,* from Issa up to the present (Hokuseido Press), Blyth somewhat explains this feeling in his introduction describing certain technical terms. *Sabi* depicts a quality of beauty tinged with loneliness, *wabi* is beauty associated with poverty, and *yugen* offers a mysterious darkness, or a religious sense.

This image-making quality invoked by Japanese poets was used as the source of several imagist experiments which ushered in much of our modern poetry. Authors such as E. Pound, T. S. Eliot, Wallace Stevens, Marianne Moore, William Carlos Williams, D. H. Lawrence, Archibald MacLeish, E. E. Cummings, and Amy Lowell tried to discard many poetry conventions and adopt some of the image-making skills of the Japanese poets. These imagists formed a cult which established specialized rules that included exactness of word, new rhythms, freedom in choice of subject, clear images, hard clear poetry, and concentration. These are the characteristics that appear in Japanese poems. A history of imagism and imagists appears in *The Imagist Poem,* Modern Poetry in Miniature, by William Pratt (E. P. Dutton & Co.). Many poems in this volume are beautiful, clear-cut gems, but somehow they lack sincerity and feeling. When Wallace Stevens speaks of "Thirteen Ways of

Nature as a Theme of Haiku
Cal State College,
Hayward, California

Looking at a Blackbird," one sees the bird in that many poses, but the poet is *looking at a blackbird*, he is not relating himself directly to it. A *haiku* poet writing of a crow would give a sense of communion, a close relationship between the bird and the writer.

One other technical characteristic of some *haiku* poetry is one that might assist young children in the creation of original poetry of their own. This characteristic is termed "Three Elements" and is explained in the volume by Yasuda. Objects in a *haiku* poem are usually located in time and place. The relationship of three essential elements appears together in one aesthetic experience. Three lines are written in such manner as to answer the question *where* on the first line, *what* on the second line, and *when* on the last one. Adapting this idea, one can arrange a *haiku* verse as, for example:

> Where? On a green lemon branch
> What? Gold hummingbirds busily
> When? Search summer's nectar.

These three lines speak of golden hummingbirds whirring above a green lemon tree questing nectar from blossoms during the summer season. Professional Oriental poets can successfully narrow down the time element to a day, an evening, or a particular instant in time.

Haiku art has many other of the intricacies of more traditional poetry, including a crystallization of experience, utilization of a common language, aspects of rhythm, alliteration, assonance, and consonance, but these are technical aspects for professional poets. Many of these qualities can be studied in the Yasuda volume. Some *haiku* verses include an ellipsis generally indicated by three periods. This refers to enlarged areas of experience not named in the poem. The Japanese writers developed a term *kire-ji* or "cutting word" to represent a well-defined thought pause related to meaning. Sometimes the "thought pause" comes at the end of the *haiku,* but usually it appears earlier in the verse. Beginners who are inexperienced in the study of Oriental forms of poetry will enjoy the clarity of *Haiku in English* by Harold G. Henderson (Charles E. Tuttle Co.).

An Historical Survey and Other Forms of Japanese Verse

Some authors have spoken of *katautas,* or a device of the question and answer, as a significant aspect of Oriental verse history. Originally, as part of spring festivals or fertility rites, the *katauta,* or question and answer, was a poetic exchange between gods and spirits. A pair of *katauta* became a poem known as the *môndô.* Later, the *môndô* was used to describe an exchange between men and men disguised as gods. The *katauta* had a syllabic pattern of five, seven, and five, or five, seven, and seven syllables varying in length from seventeen to nineteen syllables. A question was asked spontaneously and quickly. The number of seventeen or nineteen syllables probably became an established form because these were all of the syllables which a person could utter without taking a deep breath.

Another poetic form was the *sedôka* which consisted of a pair of *katautas* organized in the following syllabic pattern:

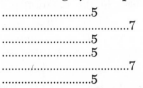

The *sedôka* was the statement of one person and was not necessarily in a question and answer form.

An extension of this pattern became the *chôka*. This had alternating lines of five and seven syllables which could continue for indefinite length until the verse was finally concluded with a line of seven syllables.

The *tanka* was a fourth form of verse. Its basic pattern was five, seven, five, seven, and seven syllables. In early *tanka* verse, one subject was discussed in the first two lines, a second subject in the second pair of lines, and a refrain, or reiteration, made up the concluding line. During a later period, a poet used the five, seven, and five pattern, or upper *hemistich*, to initiate a verse, while two syllabic lines of seven syllables each formed the concluding *hemistich*:

$$
\begin{aligned}
&............................5 \\
&....................................7 \\
&............................5 \\
&....................................7 \\
&....................................7
\end{aligned}
$$

Sometimes the initial three lines were a dependent clause or phrase, and the last two lines were an independent clause or phrase. In the second form of *tanka*, the beginning three lines were grammatically independent. Around the year A.D. 750, during the Manyô period, *tanka* poetry became quite popular. Frequently, the third line of a poem concluded with a noun.

Another form of Japanese verse was the *renga*, or linked verse. This was a poem created by two people and could extend to any length. The first person created the first *hemistich* of five, seven, and five syllables, and the partner completed the next two lines. This poem created by two persons and called the *renga*, meaning linked verse or a "duet-like poem," became the basis of the *uta-awase* or poetry tournament.

The Uta-Awase

This interesting poetry contest affected the growth of Japanese poetry greatly. During the Heian period (A.D. 794-1192), elaborate contests were held at which at least twelve hundred poems were created on different themes. Later, during the Kamakura period, three thousand poems were written at the same time. Themes were, for the most part, objects of nature.

At the *uta-awase*, participants were poets of either the right or the left. A reciter of the left-hand group read a poem and then his teammates repeated it in loud voices. A competitor on the right-hand side then read a poem and it was repeated loudly by his teammates. The left-hand side of the room supposedly took precedence over the right, because royalty and persons of noble position sat on the left side of the contest hall. Different rounds of such a contest were held, and eliminations were made. Descriptions of a *uta-awase* held in the year 913 described the attending Emperor as being clad in cedar-colored robes and dark blue trousers. The men and women sitting on the left side of the contest hall wore red robes with a cherry blossom design; those on the right side wore blue robes with a willow print. Musicians sang songs, and each contestant received an Imperial robe as a gift. Poetry subjects were early spring, cherry blossoms, the nightingale, love, and others. Objects of nature were the themes used in these contests, and the meaning of objects became more uniform. According to Yasuda, the *uta-awase* was probably responsible for the use of the seasonal theme in later *haiku* poetry.

Originally, the *hokku,* or the first three lines of a verse, was part of a five-line *tanka,* or a longer form of linked verse. Its three lines were read rapidly, for it was expected that two lines of seven syllables each would follow. Various poets established the custom of bringing the *hokku* to a compelte stop. Later, these three lines became an independent poem, or *haiku.* When these three lines became independent of longer forms, more rhythm was evident, and some pauses within the lines were made, but, originally this verse form was short enough for utterance in one breath.

Basically, the rules of the *haiku* verse form can be summarized as that it consists of seventeen syllables; it includes some reference to nature; it notes a particular event; it has an intuitive sense of an event occuring *now,* in the momentous moment of the present; it has simplicity, clarity, and compression; and its beauty lies in a grasp of a greater understanding of life through involvement with simple relationships in the natural world. In recent years, this Oriental verse in its English form has been used with many children in the United States and in Canada.

Books about Oriental Verse Patterns for Children

The teacher may wish to present some historical background and basic characteristics of Oriental poetry so that children can develop an aesthetic appreciation of this form of verse and possibly create their own personal prose poems. Several books, such as the Yasuda volume, *The Japanese Haiku,* and all of the Blyth volumes, have poetry which is beautiful and sincere enough to be understood by children in elementary school grades from volumes of this type; the teacher can select poems which have meaning to modern children, thus attuning their ears to many examples of Oriental verse before these young authors attempt to create *haiku* of their own.

Contributions of Richard Lewis

One of the compilers who has contributed much toward an interpretation of Oriental forms of poetry by children is Richard Lewis. One of his earlier books, *The Moment of Wonder,* a collection of Chinese and Japanese poetry, (Dial Press), is illustrated with paintings by Chinese and Japanese Masters. An opening section of this volume is entitled "The Family of Nature," with a poem by Issa in which a beetle rings a bell and a "hawk pirouettes." The story of breathing things is told simply and quietly.

Striking photographs by Helen Buttfield accompany three Lewis volumes. One of these, *Of This World, A Poet's Life in Poetry* (Dial Press), depicts the life and presents some of the poetry of the famous Japanese *haiku* poet, Issa. The second, a book of verses collected by Lewis, is entitled *The Wind and the Rain*, Children's Poems (Simon and Schuster). Some of the poems were taken from his book, *Miracles,* Poems by the Children of the English Speaking World (Simon and Schuster); others were published for the first time. A third Lewis volume, with photographs by Helen Buttfield, is *The Park* (Simon and Schuster). In all three books, the photographs are ones of rare beauty with accompanying words of loveliness. While the photographs do not necessarily illustrate the poems, they present images, moods, sensations, and ideas which show the relationship between poetry and the world of nature. Photographs of large shade trees, of grass reflected in a pond, of wrinkles of water running down a path, of a stormy sky, or of dripping mud puddles, give a beautiful sensation of a child's expressing his feelings for the wind, the sea, and the rain.

One of the most handsome books edited by Lewis is *Miracles* which was mentioned in the preceding paragraph. Most of the poems in this volume have been beautifully narrated by Julie Harris and Roddy McDowall on a recording entitled *Miracles* (Caedmon, T. C., 1227).

In A Spring Garden, edited by Richard Lewis, has dramatic pictures by Ezra Jack Keats (Dial Press). The illustrations show a number of effective color contrasts which heighten an awareness of *haiku* written by such traditional Japanese poets as Issa, Basho, Onitsura, Buson, Chora, Gyodai, Shiki, and Uko. Many of the poems are by Issa. One of his dramatic verses describes a giant firefly's flitting in various directions in the evening darkness. The Weston Woods Company of Connecticut has developed a filmstrip and recording, *In A Spring Garden*.

Harry Behn and Haiku Poetry

Harry Behn has edited several books about *haiku,* but his best known one is *Cricket Songs, Japanese Haiku,* with pictures selected from Sesshu and other Japanese masters (Harcourt, Brace & World). (Behn has also created poetry of his own which is part of the heritage of

childhood. His books include *Windy Morning* and *All Kinds of Time*.)
The little verses in *Cricket Songs* are simple enough for the very young
child. Behn translates poems about the spring rain, the shadow of
pines, a dead tree with an eagle's nest, a hunting sea hawk, the hoots of
an owl, a singing skylark, a leaping, tumbling river, and a baby warbler.

Aesthetics of Haiku through Film

A new experience in awareness is a moving picture film, "The Day
Is Two Feet Long," a cinematic *Haiku* conceived and directed by Peter
Rubin (The Weston Woods Company). This film visually creates the
contemplative philosophical core of verse through natural sound production and color photography. It is designed to imbue viewers with
the significance of the natural world around them. A similar type of
film which could possibly motivate the writing of poetry is "Fingal's
Cave," which shows scenes of the sea—and a gull, giving a sense of
imminence in nature. This film was produced by Avis Films.

Other Haiku Books Helpful in Creative Writing

There are a few books about *haiku* that are particularly helpful
as a means of motivating creative expression in this style. Ruby Lytle
has taken an original approach in creating *What Is the Moon?*, Japanese
Haiku Sequence (Charles E. Tuttle Co.). In this little booklet, the
author looks at the moon through the naive eyes of her Siamese kitten,
Kung-Fu-Tse. The imagery is fresh and natural as the poet speaks
of a "covey of stars" and refers to the moon as a moth. The entire
booklet is designed in black and white.

Harold G. Henderson has created two booklets which are almost
identical in content but considerably different in format. One booklet,
Haiku in English is published by the Japan Society in New York; a
second one, also *Haiku in English*, is issued by the Charles E. Tuttle Co.
These books give simple general rules of classical Japanese *haiku*. Objectives of this verse form are given, together with an excellent section
entitled "Haiku in English." The most valuable portions of these books
are the sections "Writing and Teaching Haiku." A third book by Henderson is *An Introduction to Haiku*, An Anthology of Poems and Poets
from Basho to Shiki (Doubleday & Co.—Anchor). This volume gives
biographical sketches of some of the Japanese poets as well as many
translated examples of their poems.

Birds, Frogs, and Moonlight is a child's book of *haiku* translated
by Sylvia Cassedy and Kunihiro Suetake. It is illustrated by Vo-Dinh
and the caligraphy is by Koson Okamura. Basho and Issa are well-
represented in this collection. Basho lived from 1644 until 1694, and
Issa's life spanned the years from 1762 to 1826. His mother died when
he was quite small, and he was raised by a stern stepmother whose

treatment of him is probably responsible for the sadness found in most of his poems. He himself had pity for helpless creatures. The poems in this collection are so simple that they can be understood easily by children in grades two to five.

Another recent book, 1968, is *Bug Haiku* by J. W. Hackett (Japan Publications). A Japanese poetry book for quite young children is *A Cloud of Summer,* and Other New Haiku by Doris Johnson, with illustrations by W. T. Mars (Follett Publishing Co.). Most of the pictures in this publication are delicate watercolors in pastels. The author writes of dragonflies, a gray mouse, seeds of the pomegranate, and golden chrysanthemums. A third new collection is *Silent Flowers,* a collection of Japanese *Haiku,* edited by Dorothy Price and illustrated by Nanae Ito (Hallmark Cards). Most of the verses are taken from "Haiku," Volumes I-IV, by R. H. Blyth and published by the Hokuseido Press in Tokyo, Japan. The illustrations are delicate brush strokes of natural scenes.

Peter Pauper Press Books

The Peter Pauper Press has published numerous attractive small booklets on Oriental literature. One of these is *Japanese Haiku,* 1955, translated from some of the masters of the seventeen-syllable verse form. Poets represented are Basho, Buson, Issa, Shiki, Sokan, Kikaku, Ransetsu, Joso, Yaha, and others. A second book is *Cherry Blossoms,* Japanese *Haiku*, Series III, published in 1960, which consists of translations of poems by Basho, Buson, Issa, Shiki, and others. In the introduction to this booklet, the compiler estimates that a million new *haiku* are published annually in commercial magazines. Cherry blossoms, the theme of this publication, last only three days, and the verses use this delicate flower as a symbol of the transitory quality of life. *Haiku Harvest,* Japanese *Haiku,* Series IV., published in 1962, has translations by Harry Behn and decorations by Jeff Hill. One of the most recent books published by this company is *A Haiku Garland,* a Collection of Seventeen-syllable Classic Poems, translated by Peter Beilenson, and with decorations by Jeff Hill.

The Tanka Form of Verse

Another form of verse which extends the three-line verse pattern is the *tanka.* This form has never been as popular as the *haiku.* There are two volumes containing *tanka* verse which are appropriate for children. One of these is *The Seasons of Time,* Tanka Poetry of Ancient Japan, edited by Virginia Olsen Baron and illustrated by Yashuhide Kobashi (Dial Press). These poems were originally commissioned by the Emperor of Japan and were written by poets, priests, warriors, and courtiers. The illustrator of this book has accompanied the poems with calligraphy in brush and ink drawings.

The second book, *Sounds from the Unknown,* a Collection of Japanese-American Tanka, has been translated by Lucille M. Nixon and Tomoe Tana (Alan Swallow, Publisher). The verses in this collection have been written for the most part by Japanese-Americans living in the United States and Canada.

Korean Poetry

Peter H. Lee has compiled and translated an *Anthology of Korean Poetry,* from the Earliest Era to the Present (John Day Co.). This anthology spans a period of two thousand years and contains many Korean poems which have been translated by Lee.

In an introduction to his volume, Lee writes that ancient Korean poetry was incantatory in nature. Poetry supposedly appeased the gods, kept calamities away, procured needed rain, dispersed fierce winds, and helped in recovery from diseases. Poetry, music, and dance were combined in earlier forms of Korean culture. Some poetry was perfected by the Silla people who inhabited an isolated corner of the peninsula which was not harassed by frequent foreign invasions.

Lee describes an institution known as the *hwarang* which contributed to the development of the arts. The *hwarang* was an organization composed of youths from aristocratic families. These young men vowed to sacrifice themselves for their country. In war, members of this group were mighty fighters; in peace time, they would go to the Diamond Mountains or to the coasts along the eastern sea to contemplate the beauty of nature. Members of the *hwarang* studied the classics and discussed poetry and music, and many of them composed original poems.

Music and poetry festivals, according to the author, were the "lantern" and the "harvest" celebrations which occurred on the first or second and the eleventh moons. On these occasions, people danced and sang, and eventually developed the *changga,* or long poem, which was similar in style to that of our popular ballad or folk song. A refrain at the end of each stanza expressed the mood, or tone, of this lengthy poem.

Lee states that Korean poets did not depict a stylized, stereotyped feeling toward nature, but that they reflected an "inner experience" toward the world of nature.

In the early part of the fourteenth century, the author tells us, *sijo* poetry became popular. A *sijo* was a short poem which was personal and specific, and which referred to a local subject. It sometimes ended with a witty turn of thought. Some of these poems were originally accompanied on a lute.

Sijo verse consists of three lines each of which contains fourteen to sixteen syllables; there can be no more than forty-five syllables in the total poem. This verse form has an internal division of syllables. According to Lee, the *sijo* is typically a three-line stanza, four feet to a line, and three or four syllables in a foot.

Line One - -	3	4	4	4/3
Line Two - -	3	4	4	4/3
Line Three -	3	5	4	3

During the Silla dynasty, from 57 B.C. until A.D. 935, "Master Yung-chôn created 'Song of the Comet' which presented the beautiful image of a star sweeping a path in the heavens with a 'long broomstick'" (Lee, p. 34). Much of this poetry used personification and clear imagery. In "Ode to Knight Kilbo," the moon was "an eager princess pushing her way through the heavy night sky to pursue white clouds." A pictorial metaphor compared the knight to a "towering pine" ignoring frost and snow (Lee, page 39).

Sijo poetry is more graceful in English if it is divided into six lines instead of three, with a lesser number of syllables in each line. A brief article entitled "Sijo," by Sally R. True, appearing in the March, 1966 issue of *Elementary English* includes samples of children's *sijo* verses written as part of a class project. Another article, also entitled "Sijo," by Lee Bennett Hopkins, appears in the March, 1969 *Instructor,* and contains *sijo* verses written by children.

Several interested teachers have experimented by presenting to their students the background information concerning the structure and style of Korean poetry contained in Lee's anthology. The results have been gratifying in that some of the students have enjoyed composing similar verses.

Syllabism and Other Syllabic Forms of Verse

Many forms of syllabic verse are interesting to pupils who may approach verse writing from a syllabic standpoint rather than through other formalized techniques of prosody involving scanning with formalized meter and rhyme. *Cinquain* and *lanterne* verse forms have been successfully created by elementary and junior high school pupils.

The *cinquain* is a fragile form of poetry invented by Adelaide Crapsey. It is a variant of the Japanese *tanka* verse. She composed *cinquains* in five iambic lines containing two, four, six, eight, and two syllables. Others have written *cinquains* without rhythm. The elusive charm of this form lies in its poignant imagery and unrhymed lines. A sample cinquain is "Anguish."

ANGUISH

Search now
Beneath the ruins
For hurricane victims
Dismembered by cruel raging floods —
Then weep!

Some sample *cinquains* by Adelaide Crapsey appear in *The Discovery of Poetry* by Thomas E. Sanders (Scott, Foresman and Co.).

The *lanterne* poetic form is a five-line verse shaped like a Japanese lantern with a syllabic pattern of one, two, three, four, and one syllables, respectively. It is a shaped whimsy invented by Lloyd Frank Merrell, and its beauty lies in its shape and clear-cut imagery. A sample *lanterne* follows:

Dark

Heavens

Threatening

Tropical storm

Fear!

A description of the *lanterne*, as well as several additional syllable-count forms of poetry, appears on pages 34 and 35 of *Wood's Unabridged Rhyming Dictionary* by Clement Wood (World Publishing Co.).

The author of this textbook has written three booklets which give more details about syllabic forms of poetry along with samples of children's poetry. These are "The Design of Poetry" in *Poetry for Today's Child* (F. A. Owen Publishers); "Topaz Thoughts" in *Sparkling Words: Two Hundred Practical and Creative Writing Ideas* (Wagner Printing Co.); and "Crystal Thoughts of Poetry" in *Language Sparklers for the Intermediate Grades* (Wagner Printing Co.).

Experiences with Oriental Forms of Verse

The Haiku Experience

A *haiku* experience is not a genuine one for the child unless he has had many sessions devoted to reading and listening to Oriental forms of poetry and to some of the Japanese philosophy of beauty. Many books about *haiku* have been mentioned in this chapter to aid the teacher in giving this important background. Before attempting to express themselves in the *haiku* style, children should have several encounters with nature. Undoubtedly, rural boys and girls have many opportunities to enjoy experiences with living things in the out-of-doors, but observant urban boys and girls can also find *haiku* subject matter in the city. They can, for instance, note silhouettes of multi storied buildings against a sunrise or a sunset, or they can watch the sparrows or starlings soaring in flight above the park.

Observation Experiences and Haiku

Children who live in rural areas, as well as those who are connected with an outdoor education group, can have direct encounters with nature. During the different seasons of the year, they can climb hills or mountains and collect specimens of nature. City children can visit parks, museums, or zoos and get as close to natural life as possible.

The Audubon Society, as well as the Girl Scout and the Campfire Girl organizations, issue numerous books and pamphlets on collecting natural specimens. The biology departments of many colleges maintain mounted animal and live animal collections, and catalogued plant specimen collections. The Hayward, California recreation department allows children to take home live animals in much the same way as they would check out a book from the library. The Lawrence Hall of Science, connected with the University of California, has science kits which may be rented by school classrooms for a nominal fee.

Children and adults who are interested in finding informational books about nature and science should consult the bibliography of the second edition of *Children's Literature in the Elementary School* by Charlotte S. Huck and Doris Young Kuhn (Holt, Rinehart & Winston), pages 493-506. Also, references and the conclusion of Chapter 18, "Reading for Information" in the third edition of *Children and Books* by May Hill Arbuthnot (Scott, Foresman & Co.) may be consulted as source material for Oriental nature poems. One college student, Susan Jacques, took a college level nature study course and brought collected specimens with descriptions to a fifth grade class for study. Each pupil studied the specimens carefully and then created original *haiku* verses.

Examples of Nature Study Observations from Literature

Few modern children or adults work consistently at developing their powers of observation. Great authors like Henry David Thoreau and Walt Whitman worked intently at acquiring acute observational skills.

Much of Thoreau's *Walden* is too mature for elementary school pupils, but certain paragraphs of this classic can be read to them to focus their attention upon accurate specific observations. For example, the last paragraph in "Brute Neighbors" of *Walden* precisely describes a flight of ducks. In "Housewarming" from *Walden*, Thoreau gives a meticulous description of the pond, even to minute details concerning the size of the bubbles under the surface of the ice covering the pond. He estimates that the bubbles are an eighteenth to an eighth of an inch in diameter. Brooks Atkinson has edited and written the introduction to a very fine edition, *Walden and Other Writings of Henry David Thoreau* (Random House). The reader may find helpful material on page 222 of this volume.

A paperback book, The Viking Portable Library *Walt Whitman*, selected and with notes by Mark Van Doren (Viking Press) includes many of Whitman's jottings and notations, which were written in the form of a diary. In one entry, for instance, he writes graphically about "bumblebees during the month of May." While sitting under a cherry tree, he observes the bees in their light yellow jackets "humming their perpetual rich mellow boom" (p. 20). In another section, "The Lesson of a Tree," Whitman writes in detail about all the kinds of trees which he knows (pages 600-602).

Rachel Carson describes events of the sea artistically and scientifically in three booklets which are part of the Signet Science Library. These are *The Edge of the Sea,* with illustrations by Bob Hines (New American Library of World˙Literature); *The Sea Around Us,* with drawings by Katherine L. Howe (New American Library of World Literature); and *Under the Sea Wind,* a Naturalist's Picture of Ocean Life (New American Library of World Literature). Some parts of these books are too scientific for younger children, but many poetical sections, if they are read orally, are quite understandable to intermediate grade pupils. For instance, in "The Sunless Sea" from *The Sea Around Us,* Miss Carson describes squid moving in the surface waters as luminous bubbles resembling large milky-white electric lamps being lighted and extinguished. Miss Carson's *Sense of Wonder,* with photographs by Charles Pratt (Harper & Row) is an exploration of the world of nature with a child. In this book, the author gives sensitive and artistic expression to the wonders of nature.

Enrichment Ideas Related to Oriental Poetry and Culture

Many nature books written for children, including the ones by Mary and Conrad Buff, have passages of lyrical beauty describing scenes of the great out-of-doors. The Buffs have combined their writing and illustrating talents to publish several nature books, among them *Big Tree; Elf Owl; Hurry, Skurry, and Flurry; Dash and Dart: Two Fawns;* and *Forest Folk* (Viking Press). Pupils may participate in several of the many following suggested activities related to nature, poetic expression, and Oriental culture.

Studying Natural Science and Making Field Notes: Pupils might read at least three books about some one thing in nature—bees, raccoons, hummingbirds, or sea life. They can compare different styles of authors. One of these references may be a section from a child's encyclopaedia. If possible, descriptions of animals, insects, flowers, birds, or snails, objects which are available to the child's direct experience, should be studied, because derived experiences are only secondary in nature. Notes can be taken. Pupils can then go out in the field and make observational notes and discuss their findings in "buzz sessions."

Descriptive Paragraphs: Pupils can write descriptive paragraphs on *one* object in nature that is familiar to them. This paragraph should include details such as where the object was seen, what the object was, and when it was observed. Coronet Films has issued a film, "Making Word Pictures," which helps children to write clear word images.

Writing a Haiku Verse from Questions: After pupils have studied syllabication and the syllabic pattern of *haiku,* or three lines of five, seven, and five syllables, they may wish to write a verse using the following pattern:

Where? - - - - - (5 syllables)
What? - - - - - (7 syllables)
When? - - - - - (5 syllables)

A Seasonal Word Glossary: Children might enjoy making a seasonal word glossary or dictionary. A "brainstorming" method of doing this can be fun for the pupils. The name of a season is written on the chalkboard, and the children supply words, phrases, or clauses which are related to, or descriptive of that season. The list for autumn might include:

golden	pumpkins
burnt orange	Hallowe'en
magenta red leaves	Thanksgiving
acrid odor of burning leaves	bittersweet

After the children have listened to many translated *haiku* poems, they can try to write this type of verse. They must keep in mind that a season should be either directly stated, or else inferred. The pupils can be divided into groups of three. As one child recites seasonal *haiku* poetry, the other two children record the words as if they were taking dictation.

Art Ideas and Haiku: Original *haiku* verses can be composed as a cooperative class project. The finished products may be printed in attractive calligraphy by using a Pentel, or flow brush pen. Then the children can create scenes to illustrate the *haiku* verses. One technique is to use a colored wash such as pinks, blues, and lavenders, for a background. When this is dry, Oriental type objects, such as a willow branch or a tree bursting with cherry blossoms, can be painted on the background with black ink. Or, silhouettes can be cut out of black construction paper and pasted on to the pastel painted background. Sometimes, objects of nature, such as twigs, weeds, pine cones, or pine needles, are sprayed on to the background. The border for a picture may be constructed of corrugated cardboard which is sprayed or painted. Real objects are glued to the cardboard, and a colored pastel background is used with the object in front so as to give a three-dimensional effect. A bulletin board arrangement of *haiku* verse illustrated with painted scenes can be most attractive.

Sumi-e Painting and Haiku: Sumi-e painting may be studied, after which the children can paint nature scenes using Japanese brushes and ink. *Haiku* verses may be written and illustrated with paintings of the *sumi-e* type.

Pupil Specialty Reports and a Japanese Tea: Children can prepare pupil specialty reports on various aspects of Japanese culture. These may include landscape architecture, *sumi-e* painting, or Japanese wall screens. After a period of time has been spent on Oriental culture, a Japanese tea may be given at which members of the class can read their original *haiku.*

Oriental Art and Poetry Interest Center: An interest center can be prepared after pupils have collected books about Japan, in general, and about various aspects of Japanese culture, including *haiku* and possibly *origami* (the art of Japanese paper folding), in particular. A class committee could be responsible for setting up the interest center. Books and *realia* could be placed attractively on tables above which a bulletin board might display an arrangement of *haiku* verses with examples of Oriental art. Some reproductions of classical Japanese masterpieces are available in book and art stores.

Art Museum Oriental Collections: An art museum which specializes in the display of sculpture, painting, and porcelain from the Orient might be visited. Postcard pictures or slides of the objects on display are often available at these museums. After such a visit, a report can be given in class. The Avery Brundage collection at the DeYoung Museum in San Francisco has a beautiful catalogue which describes the exhibits there.

Biographical Genre of Japanese Personages: The biographical genre should be studied, and pupils can be urged to read the biography of *Hokusai,* by Elizabeth Ripley (J. B. Lippincott Co.) or the one on Issa entitled *Of This World, A Poet's Life in Poetry* by Richard Lewis (Dial Press). Another dramatic biography is *Taller than Bandai Mountain,* The Story of Hideyo Noguchi, by Dan D'Amelio (Viking Press). This is the story of a boy who was determined to become a physician and who did become one in spite of his scarred hand. Reports on these books can be presented by the pupils.

Imagist Poetry and Haiku: Above average pupils who are interested in poetry and nature may wish to study the imagist movement in modern poetry and compare and contrast three imagist poems with three *haiku* verses.

Uta-Awase Poetry Contests: An imaginary uta-awase poetry contest can be held. This should come at the conclusion of a series of experiences with the creation of various forms of Oriental syllabic verse as translated into English. Children may wish to divide into two teams—the left and the right. Each team may select a typical symbol, such as the cherry blossom, the willow, a peony, or Fujiyama. After the contestants read or recite *haikus*, three judges may select the three best *haiku* poets.

Calligraphy and Haiku: Some *haiku* verses can be printed in neat calligraphy on a scroll made by fastening a piece of bamboo or a thin stick, painted black, to each end of a piece of Japanese rice paper or colored tissue paper. Illustrations can be pasted at the sides of the printed poems. An interesting book by Juliet Kreps entitled *Birds* (Walker & Co.), shows abstract calligraphy in the style of Japanese writing masters.

Stick Figure Shadowgraphs: A heavy cardboard box placed on a table may be used for the shadowgraph stage. Scenery can be made out of construction paper and pasted to the sides of the box. Color can be obtained by cutting holes in parts of the scenery and fastening colored cellophane over them. Pupils can cut out silhouette figures of the actors—perhaps a Japanese philosopher, a poet, or a lovely lady. Simple shadowgraph figures can be made from stiff dark paper or

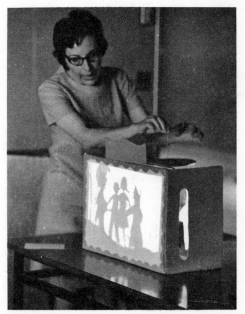

Oriental Shadowgraphs and Haiku
Evelyn N. Schneider
Cal-State College,
Hayward, California

cardboard. Figures can be cut or torn into a simple shape with wire or wooden supports attached with glue, staples, or cello tape. A blanket can be draped below the stage to hide the puppet manipulators. Light from a slide projector or from bulbs in a holder can be placed either above or behind the scene in order to form the shadow. Japanese music played on a recorder can provide the mood or tone for the play. As the children manipulate the actor-figures through the use of either attached sticks or stiff wires, they can recite poetry, either their own original *haiku* verses or the poems of traditional Japanese poets. Three sources on shadow puppets are A. C. Scott's *The Puppet Theater of Japan* (Charles E. Tuttle Co.); *Shadow Puppets* by Olive Blackham, (Harper & Row); and Stuart and Patricia Robinson's *Exploring Puppetry* (Taplinger Publishing Co.).

Composing Linked Haiku Verses: In a volume, *Catch Me A Wind* by Patricia Hubbell (Atheneum Publishers), the poet composes seven poems, entitled "Haiku for a Week in Spring." After reading these chained or linked poems, pupils can experiment with seven verses such as "Haiku for a Week in Fall" or "Haiku for a Week in Winter." Painted illustrations can accompany each verse.

Creating Tanka Poetry: The tanka form of verse follows the five, seven, five, seven, and seven syllabic pattern. After reading some *tanka* verses in references cited in this chapter or from other sources, pupils can work as partners. One pupil may initiate a *tanka* by asking a question and phrasing it in five, seven, and five syllables. His partner can answer in two lines of seven syllables each. This technique of working as partners was used when poets created the *renga* form of linked verse.

Nature Photographs and Oriental Verse: Richard Lewis has cooperated with a professional photographer, Helen Buttfield, in creating the volumes, *The Wind and the Rain* and *The Park* (Simon and Schuster). After looking through these books, the pupils can choose a theme and follow through by taking a series of black and white photographs to portray this theme. Then their original *haiku* or *tanka* verse can correlate with the photographs. Some children may prefer to take colored slides. If so, the verses can be tape-recorded or printed on colored four by six inch cards and numbered. The cards could be joined together with curtain rings to form a little booklet. The slides can be placed in sequence in a magazine loader and, as they are changed, the cards accompanying each slide can be read and then flipped over.

An Activity with "In a Spring Garden" (Richard Lewis): The teacher can present the film strip, *In a Spring Garden,* produced by The Weston Woods Company, or she could show the beautiful pictures from the book of that title, edited by Richard Lewis and illustrated by Ezra Jack Keats. These pictures might stimulate the children to create illustrations for their own original *haiku* verses or for some of the poems written by Issa or Buson. An interesting media for these illustrations is soap flake finger painting. Proportions are 7 cups of water, 1½ cups of starch, and 1½ cups of soap flakes. The starch is mixed with cold water to form a paste. Boiling water is then added until the mixture is glossy. The soap flakes are stirred into the mixture while it it still warm. When it is cool, powdered tempera paint is added. Another media is wallpaper paste finger paint. The proportions for this are 3 parts of water to 1 part of powdered wallpaper paste with some tempera paint to give the mixture color.

A Haiku Motion Picture Experience: The motion picture film, "The Day is Two Feet Long" (Weston Woods Company) can be projected, and pupils can create original verse while the mood of quiet beauty and loveliness is being experienced.

Chinese Poetry: Translated Chinese verse has not been adapted so as to become popular with younger children. However, the primary teacher may wish to introduce some of the poems from *The Rapier of Lu, Patriot Poet of China,* with translations and biography by Clara M. Candlin (Mrs. W. T. Young) and John Murray. Lu Yu was a patriotic poet who lived during the Southern Sung Dynasty in the twelfth and early thirteenth centuries. When invaders occupied much Chinese territory, Lu Yu urged his countrymen to rise up and free China from the oppressors. He was also known as Lu Fang Weng.

Several of this poet's verses are warlike and more suited to older people, but a section in this book entitled "Nature" has many beautiful selections that may appeal to small children. In the poem, "I Stand Alone," Lu writes about grief and solitude, and hills "devouring" the setting sun. His "Song of the River Moon" presents a beautiful image of an old man looking back, feeling cramped by artificial court life, and longing for a solitary stork to carry him beneath its wing to Fairyland. In "Summer Commences," the poet longs for a world of peace where the cuckoo calls and a road winds between the hemp and trees of mulberry. Children may be inspired to draw illustrations for some of these Chinese poems which are at their experiential level.

Creative Stitchery and Chinese Symbolism: After studying the symbolism in Japanese poetry, pupils may be interested in symbolism used by the Chinese people. Ferdinand Lessing has published a volume, *Chinese Symbolism in Art* (University of California Press). The author shows that each flower or animal used in Chinese art has a symbolic meaning. Spring is symbolized by the dragon, giving the spirit of life's renewal. Winter is shown by the old tortoise. Summer is the brilliant phoenix, and autumn is represented by the white tiger, symbolizing courageous action. The peony is the flower of spring; the lotus stands for summer; the chrysanthemum means autumn; and the plum blossom represents winter. The teacher may wish to obtain the Lessing volume and go into more detail about Chinese symbolism. During the period of celebration of the Chinese New Year, members of the class can investigate the significance of symbols in art and culture. Children may develop a Chinese symbol design and transfer a piece of it to cloth, after which it can be worked in some form of creative stitchery.

SELECTED REFERENCES FOR CHILDREN

BARON, VIRGINIA OLSEN, ed. *The Seasons of Time,* Tanka Poetry of Ancient Japan. Illustrated by Yashuhide Kobashi. New York: Dial Press, 1968.

BEHN, HARRY, trans. *Haiku Harvest,* Japanese Haiku, Series IV. Decorations by Jeff Hill. Mount Vernon, N. Y.: Peter Pauper Press, 1962.

————. *Cricket Songs, Japanese Haiku.* Pictures selected from Sesshu and other Japanese Masters. New York: Harcourt, Brace & World, 1964.

BEILENSON, PETER, trans. *A Haiku Garland,* a Collection of Seventeen-Syllable Classic Poems. Decorations by Jeff Hill. Mount Vernon, N. Y.: Peter Pauper Press, 1968.

BUFF, MARY and CONRAD. *Big Tree.* New York: Viking Press, 1946, 1963.

————. *Hurry, Skurry, and Flurry.* New York: Viking Press, 1954.

————. *Dash and Dart: Two Fawns.* New York: Viking Press, 1942.

————. *Forest Folk.* New York: Viking Press, 1962.

BUFF, MARY MARSH. *Elf Owl.* Illustrated by Conrad Buff. New York: Viking Press, 1958.

CASSEDY, SYLVIA, and SUETAKE, KUNIHIRO, trans. *Birds, Frogs and Moonlight.* Illustrated by Vo-Dinh. Calligraphy by Koson Okamura. Garden City, N. Y.: Doubleday & Co., 1967.

Cherry Blossoms, Japanese Haiku, Series III. Translations of poems by Basho, Buson, Issa, Shiki, and others. Mount Vernon, N. Y.: Peter Pauper Press, 1960.

COATSWORTH, ELIZABETH. *The Cat Who Went to Heaven.* Illustrated by Lynd Ward. New York: Macmillan Co., 1958.

D'AMELIO, DAN. *Taller than Bandai Mountain.* The story of Hideyo Noguchi. Illustrated by Fred Banbery. New York: Viking Press, 1968.

HACKETT, J. W. *Bug Haiku.* Illustrated by Earl Thollander. New York: Japan Publications, 1968.

HUBBELL, PATRICIA. *Catch Me a Wind.* New York: Atheneum Publishers, 1968.

In a Spring Garden, film strip and recording PRP 113. Weston, Conn.: The Weston Woods Co.

Japanese Haiku. Mount Vernon, N. Y.: Peter Pauper Press, 1955.

JOHNSON, DORIS. *A Cloud of Summer* and Other New Haiku. Illustrations by W. T. Mars. Chicago: Follett Publishing Co., 1967.

KREPS, JULIET. *Birds.* Foreword by Philip Hofer. New York: Walker & Co., 1968.

LAGERLOF, SELMA. *The Wonderful Adventure of Nils.* Narrated with pictures by Hans Malmberg and translated by Richard E. Oldenburg. Stockholm, Sweden: Victor Petterson's Bokindustri A. B., 1967.

LARRICK, NANCY, selected by. *Green Is Like a Meadow of Grass,* An Anthology of Children's Pleasure in Poetry. Drawings by Kelly Oechsli. Champaign, Ill.: Garrard Publishing Co., 1968.

LEWIS, RICHARD. *Miracles.* Poems by Children of the English Speaking World. New York: Simon and Schuster, 1966.

—————, ed. *In a Spring Garden.* Pictures by Ezra Jack Keats. New York: Dial Press, 1965.

—————. *The Moment of Wonder,* a Collection of Chinese and Japanese Poetry. Illustrated with paintings by Chinese and Japanese Masters. New York: Dial Press, 1964.

—————. *Of This World, A Poet's Life in Poetry.* Photographs by Helen Buttfield. New York: Dial Press, 1968.

—————. Collected by. *The Wind and the Rain,* Children's Poems. Photographs by Helen Buttfield. New York: Simon and Schuster, 1968.

—————. *The Park.* Photographs by Helen Buttfield. New York: Simon and Schuster, 1968.

LYTLE, RUBY. *What Is the Moon?* Japanese Haiku Sequence. Rutland, Vermont: Charles E. Tuttle Co., 1965.

NIXON, LUCILLE M., and TOMOE TANA, trans. *Sounds from the Unknown,* a Collection of Japanese-American Tanka. Denver: Alan Swallow, Publisher, 1964.

PRATT, WILLIAM. *The Imagist Poem,* Modern Poetry in Miniature. New York: E. P. Dutton & Co., 1965.

PRICE, DOROTHY, ed. *Silent Flowers,* a Collection of Japanese Haiku. Illustrated by Nanae Ito. New York: Hallmark Cards, 1967.

REXROTH, KENNETH. *One Hundred Poems from the Japanese.* New York: New Directions, Publisher, 1964.

RIPLEY, ELIZABETH. *Hokusai,* a Biography. Philadelphia: J. B. Lippincott Co., 1968.

RUBIN, PETER, conceived and directed by. "The Day is Two Feet Long," a cinematic Haiku. Weston, Conn.: Weston Woods Co.

STEWART, HAROLD. *A Net of Fireflies,* an anthology of 320 haiku of Japan with 33 haiku paintings in color. Rutland, Vermont: Charles E. Tuttle Co.

VIZENOR, GERALD ROBERT. *Raising the Moon Vines,* Original Haiku. Minneapolis: Nodin Press, 1968.

—————. *Empty Swings,* Haiku in English, with calligraphy by Haruko Isobe. Minneapolis: Nodin Press, 1967.

—————. *Seventeen Chirps.* Minneapolis: Nodin Press, 1968.

SELECTED REFERENCES FOR PROFESSIONALS AND ADULTS

ARBUTHNOT, MAY HILL. *Children and Books.* 3d ed. Glenview, Ill.: Scott, Foresman & Co., 1964.

ATKINSON, BROOKS, edited and with introduction by. *Walden and Other Writings of Henry David Thoreau.* New York: Modern Library, a division of Random House, 1950.

BLACKHAM, OLIVE. *Shadow Puppets.* London: Barrie & Rockliff, 1960. New York: Harper & Row, Publishers, 1962.

BLYTH, R. H. *Haiku,* Vol. I., Eastern Culture; Vol. II., *Spring*; Vol. III., *Summer-Autumn*; Vol. IV., *Autumn-Winter*. Tokyo, Japan: Hokuseido Press, 1966.

——————. *A History of Haiku*, from Issa Up to the Present. Tokyo, Japan: The Hokuseido Press, 1964.

CANDLIN, CLARA M., translations and biography by. *The Rapier of Lu, Patriot Poet of China*. London: John Murray, 1946.

CARLSON, RUTH KEARNEY. *Poetry for Today's Child*. New York: F. A. Owen Publishers, 1968.

——————. *Sparkling Words: Two Hundred Practical and Creative Writing Ideas*. Berkeley: Wagner Printing Co., 1968.

——————. *Language Sparklers for the Intermediate Grades*. Berkeley: Wagner Printing Co., 1968.

CARSON, RACHEL. *The Edge of the Sea*. Illustrations by Bob Hines. New York: New American Library of World Literature, 1955.

——————. *The Sea Around Us*. Drawings by Katherine L. Howe. New York: New American Library of World Literature, 1961.

——————. *Under the Sea Wind*, a Naturalist's Picture of Ocean Life. New York: New American Library of World Literature, 1955.

——————. *Sense of Wonder*. Photographs by Charles Pratt. New York: Harper & Row, Publishers, 1956.

HENDERSON, HAROLD G. *Haiku in English*. New York: Japan Society, 250 Park Avenue, New York 10017, 1967.

——————. *Haiku in English*. Rutland, Vermont: Charles E. Tuttle Co., 1967.

——————. *An Introduction to Haiku*, An Anthology of Poems and Poets from Basho to Shiki. Garden City, N. Y.: Doubleday & Co.—Anchor, 1958.

HOPKINS, LEE BENNETT. "Sijo." *The Instructor*, March, 1969.

HUCK, CHARLOTTE S., and KUHN, DORIS YOUNG. *Children's Literature in the Elementary School*. 2d ed. New York: Holt, Rinehart & Winston, 1968.

KEENE, DONALD. *Japanese Literature*, an Introduction to Western Readers. New York: Grove Press, 1955.

LEE, PETER H., comp. and trans. *Anthology of Korean Poetry*, from the Earliest Era to the Present. New York: John Day Co., 1964.

LESSING, FERDINAND. *Chinese Symbolism in Art*. Berkeley: University of California Press, 1935.

OBATA, CHIURA. *Sumi-e*. Tokyo, Japan: Daiichi Seihan Co., distributed by Chiura Obata, 2430 Oregon Street, Berkeley, California 94705.

ROBINSON, STUART and PATRICIA. *Exploring Puppetry*. New York: Taplinger Publishing Co., 1967.

SANDERS, THOMAS E. *The Discovery of Poetry*. Glenview, Ill.: Scott, Foresman & Co., 1967.

SCOTT, A. C. *The Puppet Theater of Japan*. Rutland, Vermont: Charles E. Tuttle Co., 1963.

TRUE, SALLY R. "Sijo." *Elementary English* 43:245-246, March, 1966.

VAN DOREN, MARK, selected and with notes by. *Walt Whitman*. New York: The Viking Portable Library, Viking Press, 1955.

WATTS, ALAN W. *The Way of Zen*. New York: Pantheon Books, 1957.

WOOD, CLEMENT. *Wood's Unabridged Rhyming Dictionary*. Cleveland: World Publishing Co., 1943.

YASUDA, KENNETH. *The Japanese Haiku*, Its Essential Nature, History, and Possibilities in English, with Selected Examples. Rutland, Vermont: Charles E. Tuttle Co., 1966.

chapter 4

the many faces
of aloneness

Books Using Loneliness as a Theme

As one reads many novels written for older elementary school children, he finds certain themes that set the tone for the narrative structure of those novels. The loneliness of man struggling to survive against nature's powerful forces and the conflicts of human beings with animals or with each other are frequent themes in literature for adolescents. Loneliness takes many facets.

Loneliness Fosters Courage and Ingenuity: Somehow, man experiences a sense of aloneness when he stands on a mountain peak and views the land below. He is facing himself as well as an environment from which he can win survival. Poetry and prose often reflect this poignantly beautiful feeling of loneliness; but there are also some novels and biographies for young adolescents that give this sense of aloneness, as well as an admiration for those who have conquered the elements which are both beautiful and terrible.

Several novels and biographies depict this great feeling of loneliness, coupled with native ingenuity. *The Monarch of Juan Fernandez* by Martin Ballard (Charles Scribner's Sons) describes Alexander Selkirk who was the inspiration for Daniel Defoe, creator of the *Life and Strange Surprising Adventures of Robinson Crusoe*. The Ballard novel, written for children twelve years or older, tells how Selkirk was forced to live by his wits in order to attain survival when he was left alone on Juan Fernandez Island with only an old sea chest, his mother's Bible, some salt biscuits, tinned meat, and a little ammunition. He learned how terrible it is to endure a forced feeding of turtle and crayfish boiled in tepid water. Selkirk's ingenuity in making usable clothes and implements helped him to survive. And he saw how important companionship is even though the companions are only wild goats which go leaping over crags and rocks, or some cats who had been left behind from old sea vessels. The entire novel is exciting, but Chapter 2, "Monarch of All He Surveyed," gives an intense feeling of loneliness and isolation. Here, the reader senses the fear of darkness and of the unknown dangers that lurk on the island's mountainside. It is suggested that one of the editions of *Robinson Crusoe* be read so that parallel events and other resemblances between the two books can be noted.

A similar novel is one concerning the ingenuity, courage, and loneliness of an Indian maiden, Karana, in *Island of the Blue Dolphins* by Scott O'Dell (Houghton Mifflin Co.). Karana, the Indian girl known as The Girl with the Long Black Hair, lived alone on the Island of San Nicholas from 1835 until 1853 and is recorded in history as The Lost Woman of San Nicholas. She had to overcome her inbred tribal taboos and superstitions in order to provide food for survival. She clothed herself in cormorant feathers, and her loneliness was so desperate that she tamed wild dogs as her companions. She is a female Robinson Crusoe who is greatly admired by her readers. Chapter 19 of this novel depicts a tremendous struggle between Karana and a giant devilfish, a struggle which was hindered by the impetuousity of her dog, Rontu. The diction is restrained and simple, but one can almost feel the flailing agonies of the giant suckered fish twisting his many arms around Karana and can sense the quiet desperation of the lonely girl struggling for her life.

Another novel by Scott O'Dell, *The Black Pearl* (Houghton Mifflin Co.), gives a beautiful portrayal of courage and religious faith when these virtues are confronted by superstition. As the story unfolds, we meet Ramon Salazar who is a new partner in his father's pearl fishing business. All of his life he has been threatened by the supposed dangers and superstitions surrounding the Manta Diablo whose mouth, it was said, had seven rows of teeth like knives with sharp steel blades. Some people believed that its claws would grab the unwary ones and that its forked tongue might breathe fire. When young Ramon discovers the Black Pearl, the most valuable pearl in the world, the superstitious natives fear that Manta Diablo is angry, because unfortunate events begin to happen in the pearl fishing village. The plot thickens as we learn that the Sevillano also covets the great pearl. Subsequent exciting and dangerous incidents involve Ramon and the crafty diver at the island of Los Muertos, and in the waters near Baja, California. Much of this novel is reminiscent of *The Pearl* by John Steinbeck (Viking Press) and of *The Old Man and the Sea* by Ernest Hemingway (Charles Scribner's Sons).

A third novel by O'Dell, entitled *The King's Fifth* (Houghton Mifflin Co.), is more complex in its structure. The novelist takes the reader back and forth in time and location. We first meet Esteban Sandoval in the year 1541 at the Fortress of San Juan de Ulúa where he is recording his thoughts in a diary. The scene then shifts to the land of the conquistadors where Esteban, along with Captain Mendoza and Father Francisco, have many adventures in their quest for gold in the Indian cities of Chicilticale, Hawikuh, Nexpan, and Tawhi. The plot develops when the Royal Audiencia brings charges against young Sandoval, the cartographer of an expedition, inasmuch as the King demands one-fifth of all the gold hidden in Cibola. The reader is taken back to the Fortress of San Juan de Ulúa where the boy, Esteban, spends many lonely hours awaiting the verdict of the Audiencia. Finally, he lives out three years of imprisonment in his fortress prison cell.

The author aptly depicts the lure of gold as a fever to adventurers, many of whom resort to all kinds of ruthless means against both fellow adventurers and the Indians, to get a larger hoard of gold. At times O'Dell writes colorfully and tersely as he compares the scorching sun to "a leech sucking out moisture from the flesh of parched travellers." Or, the sound of the sea resembles "the dryness of a knife carving out silken cloth." Zia, the Indian girl interpreter who accompanies the expedition, "gazes with an obsidian-eyed expression." The aged, decrepit judges of the Royal Audiencia sit "with faces the color of the underneath side of a sturgeon." This is an adventure novel based on historical facts, but it probably will be enjoyed more by older adolescents who have had some background in Spanish American history.

A novel which can easily accompany the reading of *The King's Fifth* is *Walk the World's Rim* by Betty Baker (Harper & Row), because the basic plots are somewhat similar. This is a story of the expedition of Cabeza de Vaca as seen through the eyes of Chakoh, an Indian lad who lives in the poverty-stricken Texas hill country. This novel has many themes—superstition, slavery, a conflict of mores, poverty, differences in religion, cupidity, friendship, and fear. An important theme is slavery as depicted through the characterization of Esteban, a Negro slave. Chakoh discovers that the white man's God is somewhat different from his Spirit of Misfortune. Esteban helps the Indian lad to comprehend that the world is round and that man is walking around it "like an ant treading on the rim of a basket." Three Spanish soldiers—Cabeza de Vaca, Dorantes, and Castillo greedily seek gold in the seven cities of Cibola and have little compassion for the natives or for Esteban, the slave who sees promises as a mirage from afar.

Ishi, Last of His Tribe by Theodora Kroeber, and with drawings by Ruth Robbins (Parnassus Press) is a somewhat different tale. It is told in the first person by Ishi, who, as last of his tribe, is the lonely survivor of a small band of California Indians of the Yahi tribe which formerly lived near the foothills below Mount Lassen. Most of the tribal members flee to the mountains to conceal themselves from gold seekers and settlers. Here the tribal people use moral and spiritual courage to survive against an alien world. In 1911, Ishi is discovered in the corral of a slaughter house near Oroville. He is the last survivor of his tribe and is brought to the museum of anthropology of the University of California located on Parnassus Heights in San Francisco. Here he lives until his death in 1916.

Theodora Kroeber writes compassionately of Ishi and his people. Many portions of this book are poetical in style and feeling. The morning sun waves its "colored plumes high into the Sky World," and the New Year is the period of the "green clover moon." Timawi and Ishi rush to a creek and raise up two twisting salmon "gleaming with colors of the moon." Ancient Yahi songs are sung occasionally in this tale, but the songs dreamed by Ishi are poetically expressed and cleverly printed in italics. This novel device clearly separates the dream from reality and gives the inner thoughts of Ishi. A book for adults, on the same subject, by Theodora Kroeber is *Ishi in Two Worlds,* a biography of the last wild Indian in North America (University of California Press).

A somewhat similar theme is treated in *The Wrath of Coyote* by Jean Montgomery (William Morrow & Co.). Kotola, an old man, tells about his life as a Miwok Indian whose tribe had lost the battle for survival against Spanish missionaries and Indians as these visitors to his land had brought cruelty, disease, and death. The book includes a glossary of Miwok words.

Resourcefulness and a feeling for the out-of-doors is evident in *My Side of the Mountain* which was written and illustrated by Jean Craighead George (E. P. Dutton & Co.). The author tells of a New York boy who leaves his family and goes to the mountain wilderness for a year to prove that he can maintain his personal independence. His house is a hemlock tree, and his lamp consists of a turtle shell with deer fat for fuel. His clothes are deer skins, and flour comes from acorns. The boy shows much resourcefulness and ingenuity as he reaches maturity.

Man has always sought the companionship of others in his struggles for survival against the wilderness, and the early cave man, or Neanderthal creature, frequently faced loneliness and privation with terror and, at the same time, with bravery.

Leonard Wibberley has created a fascinating adventure story in *Attar of the Ice Valley* (Farrar, Straus & Giroux). Here is a story of bravery, superstition, and hardship against a background of crude ice-bound walls similar to those of Greenland. Tribes are small, sometimes consisting of only four or five persons. Old Huru is the leader of the tribe about whom this story is written. He helps his tribesmen as best he can, but it is evident that man living in rocky caves with crude stones and sticks for weapons has to stand on his own legs. The hunter is also the hunted, and dark spirits breathe icy breaths. Attar, one of the tribesmen, kills the blue citti with its soft silver fur, but he longs for fur from the wolf or the bear. His sticks, stabbing spear, and a knife chipped from a green stone are all the weapons that he has to attack a pack of dungoes, dangerous enemies of men. It is interesting to note that while both dungoes and men suffer from fear, man does not show it. Attar feels braver and less lonely when the members of his tribe call him the new warrior, hunter of dungoes.

Gurth, another tribesman, is feared because he is a hunter who kills for sport rather than for sustenance. It is the law of the tribe that no one kills more than is needed lest the country become bare of food leaving all to die of hunger. As the story progresses, superstitious tribal members feel that Attar has offended Great Bear. As a result, he becomes an outcast from his own people, and no one even offers him food and water at night.

During his loneliness and need, Attar encounters a dungo dog that is badly wounded, but since it does not bare its fangs, a friendship develops between the two as they lie down together for mutual warmth. In the morning, Attar finds the dungo hungrily chewing his cloak, but his loss is offset by the realization that the wild dog could easily have slashed him to death.

Then Mikedoo, the dungo, and Attar together kill the rua, thus supplying meat for the people, and thereafter, the dog and man hunt together against other wildnerness beasts. Huru and Attar decide to hunt for a land beyond the valley of ice. They encounter volcanic lava and also face the terrors of the sea with waves rising higher and higher.

The Loneliness of Insanity

Another form of loneliness is insanity, a loss of sense which logical men cannot understand. One of many novels on this subject is *The Dark Canoe* by Scott O'Dell (Houghton Mifflin Co.). The story is told from the viewpoint of Nathan who sails from Nantucket with his older brothers, Caleb and Jeremy, to try to discover what caused the strange loss of the *Amy Foster*. As mysterious events develop, Caleb becomes a victim of madness, an obsession that he is Ahab of *Moby Dick* in quest of the mysterious white whale. This novel has much symbolism and aludes frequently to parallel events in the great Melville masterpiece. Even the coffee-colored dark canoe can be compared with the fragile quality of life itself.

A novel focused on loneliness, insanity, and the problems of growing into maturity is *Up a Road Slowly* by Irene Hunt (Follett Publishing Co.). Upon the death of her mother, Julie has within herself a feeling of bewilderment and desolation, and she expresses her frustrations in hysterical screaming. Half afraid, but also somewhat fascinated, she hides in a closet under the stairs in Aunt Cordelia's house. Here, like a bewildered animal licking its wounds in solitude, she rests against a pile of bedding, preferring loneliness to companionship with other children. Eventually, Julie develops compassion for Aggie, a mistreated, undernourished, retarded girl who flounders helplessly through the pages of a reader. Later, Julie becomes enmeshed in the affairs of the Jonathan Eltwings, and as she observes the gradual mental decline of Kathy Eltwing, she is puzzled over the eeriness of this illness called insanity. Still later, she again experiences loneliness after her burned-out love affair with Brett. Climbing "up a road slowly" to a beautiful understanding of some of the deeper meanings of life, Julie matures into a lovely woman with hope for a calmer future.

Loneliness in the Far North

An awesome experience with the dangers and violence of glacial mountains is portrayed in *Akavak: an Eskimo Journey* by James A. Houston, with illustrations by the author, (Harcourt, Brace & World). A boy and his grandfather undertake a perilous journey to reach the home of the elder one's brother. The two travellers suffer cold and hunger in their hazardous trek. Extreme loneliness and despair is felt by the boy when the old man dies as a result of the terrible experience. The Canadian author has also written *The White Archer: an Eskimo Legend*, and *Tita'liktak: an Eskimo Legend* (Harcourt, Brace & World).

Another tale of Arctic climes is *Elli of the Northland* by Margaret Ruthin (Farrar, Straus & Giroux). This is a story of a Lapland girl, fourteen-year-old Elli, who lives the life of a Nomadic reindeer herder. She and her family have a reverence for nature. Much family conflict ensues when Elli discovers that Kirsti and Jussa are not her grandparents. Much of the novel concerns the quiet resourcefulness of a girl trained to survive a hardy life against frightening perils.

A similar story for young children about love and courage in the far north of Alaska is *Inatuk's Friend*, written and illustrated by Suzanne Stark Morrow (Little, Brown and Co.). *Orphan of the Tundra* by Verne T. Davis (Weybright & Talley) reveals the great ingenuity and courage of a boy who undertakes a lonely trek to the Arctic Northlands to deliver Wonly, the musk ox, to its Arctic home. Tom has raised the musk ox from the time it was an injured and abandoned calf, but the animal has become too dangerous for civilized life, and the boy can not bear to have it confined behind the bars of zoo cages.

A tale of fortitude and ingenuity is *The Story of Comock, the Eskimo* as told to Robert Flaherty, edited by Edmund Carpenter, (Simon and

Schuster). In 1902, Comock takes his starving family across frozen ice to an island in search of game. He has only a knife and a few stones for tools and weapons, but during their ten years on the island, Comock learns to use walrus tusks for sled runners, and he fashions harpoons and needles out of ivory. After their ten years of privation, Comock and his family return to the Hudson Bay outpost at Cape Wolstenholme in a boat made of driftwood and whalebone. The boat is kept from capsizing by inflated seal bladders. Comock and his family are clothed in animal skins and duck feathers.

A novel somewhat in this same vein is *Kavik, the Wolf Dog* by Walt Morey (E. P. Dutton & Co.). This is the saga of a wolf dog that is rescued by fifteen-year-old Andy Evans who finds the animal amidst the wreckage of a plane accident on a remote Alaskan mountain. This book won the 1968 Dutton Junior Animal Book award.

Novels of Loneliness and Isolation

Several recent books show an intense loneliness which so overpowers the principal character that he feels isolated from the rest of humanity. A beauitfully poetic novel for younger children is *Su An* by Doris Johnson (Follett Publishing Co.). Little Su An lives in a Korean orphanage where she is treated kindly enough, but the child is always dreaming of her mother who might be alive and who might some day come to take her home. She is reluctant to be adopted by American parents lest this be a barrier to a reunion with the real mother of her dreams. In poetic prose, the author compares the wind to "a tiger switching its tail," and "a kiss seems as light as a dragonfly's wing."

A rather unusual story is *A Year to Grow* by Felice Holman (W. W. Norton & Co.). The girl in this novel is sent to the Mary Barrows School to grow up in its quiet dreariness. There are the usual stereotypes of boarding school characters and their pranks. In the depths of her isolation and loneliness, the girl visits a graveyard which is neglected and overgrown with weeds. She decides to beautify it and, whenever she can steal away from her classmates, she feverishly digs out the weeds. Tenderly, she decorates the graves and sweeps them with a hairbrush so that the buttercups, daisies, and clover can be seen.

In the graveyard, she meets Dr. Duncan's son, Jimmy, who frequently eludes his parents and his nurses. The boy cannot read, and he seems to be mentally retarded, but he listens intently when she reads beautiful poetry to him. He helps her tend the graves, and as they share their tasks, some of the girl's isolation and loneliness disappear. It is not until she hears of Jimmy's death that she realizes that he has been suffering from a long and disabling illness, but she is comforted in the knowledge that he will never suffer again.

A third unusual book of loneliness might be termed a photographic narrative. *It's Wings that Make Birds Fly, the Story of a Boy* (Pantheon Books) is a narrative about a child, Otis Bennett, who is a composite character, one who could come either from Harlem or from the Watts district. We see Otis wandering alone near grubby store fronts and in trash-filled alleys. His father and mother are separated, and the boy, feeling deep loneliness, wants desperately to have his parents back together again. The complete book, in which the inner feelings of a Negro boy are sensitively portrayed, is the result of a series of taped conversations recorded by Sandra Weiner. It would probably be enjoyed more by adults and by students in child development courses than by children of the peer culture.

A fourth novel of this type has an Australian setting. *Boy Alone* by Reginald Ottley (Harcourt, Brace & World) tells of a lonely boy who is a "wood-and-water-joey" at the site of an Australian cattle station. Workers at the station mean to be friendly, but life at the outback is hard. Exciting, but often dangerous occurrences take place constantly, among them the wild, and almost disastrous, charge of a bull; dust storms with their accompanying raw-red darkness; the painful bite of a centipede; and the uncertain but precarious ever-presence of rattlesnakes. The boy encounters one of his life's hardest moments when, after it has been decided that only one pup from Brolga's litter can be kept, he is forced to bury the other new-born puppies. His dog, Rags, is a needed companion, and one more beloved by him than any human being. In desperation at the possibility of losing his dog, the boy escapes to the sandhills where he is found by Kanga, an old man who has had a life of sun, dust, and loneliness. In the end, however, Kanga comes to understand the quiet desperation of the boy and allows him to have the joy of possessing a creature of his own—his dog, Rags.

Another novel dealing with loneliness, as well as with dire poverty and the many difficulties that are a natural consequence of having a physical deformity is *Taller than Bandai Mountain, the Story of Hideyo Noguchi,* by Dan D'Amelio (The Viking Press). This is the biography of Noguchi, a renowned Japanese scientist who conducted research on snake venom; on microorganisms such as spirochetes which are the known cause of syphilis; on blood parasites which cause Oroya fever; and on other diseases and their causes. He died in Africa while doing research on yellow fever. The biography stresses Noguchi's overwhelming desire to become a doctor, and it tells about his apprenticeship with Dr. Watanabe. He was tortured by his fellow students, both in Tokyo and in his own village. His affliction was a burn-scarred hand, and he spent hours of loneliness trying to overcome the difficulties he encountered whenever he tried to use the hand.

A famous person who spent much of his life in loneliness was Henry Morton Stanley, adventurous newspaper man, author, and explorer of darkest Africa. A fascinating biography by Fredrika Shumway Smith is *Stanley, African Explorer* (Rand McNally & Co.). Misery and aloofness from his fellowman characterize the boy hero as the biography opens. He has been deserted by his parents, and at St. Asaph's Workhouse, he is beaten unmercifully by the half-insane master. Discouraged and heartsick, he leaves the workhouse. During his desperate wanderings, he meets a ship's officer who hires him as a crew member of the *Windermere*. His voyage takes him to the United States where he becomes slightly involved in the Civil War, writing dispatches from the war front.

The great turning point of Stanley's life is his meeting with James Gordon Bennett who sends him to Central Africa to try to find Dr. David Livingstone. When he discovers the explorer in darkest Africa, Stanley utters the now famous words, "Dr. Livingstone, I presume?"

Suffering the tortures of jungle fever, the animosities of the natives, and the lack of finances, Stanley nevertheless explores the whole length of the Congo River and lays the foundation for the Congo Free State. He penetrates into the equatorial forests of the "Dark Continent" and finally discovers the cataracts of the almost two hundred feet high Stanley Falls.

The explorer sickly turns away when he sees unhappy natives being captured by Arab slave traders who slaughter all who try to escape. Burned, blackened traces of ruined primitive dwellings, darkened stakes, burned out banana groves, and scorched palms offer evidence of the Arabs' cruelty.

Stanley finds some happiness in his life of adventure, but at times he feels friendless and homeless, and his ceaseless wanderings are probably fostered by his unhappy loneliness. Rarely does he hold firm friendships, for his restless spirit allows him to linger only briefly in one place.

Stanley is almost alone in championing his geographical discoveries, for the British Royal Geographical Society refuses to believe that the Lualaba River is the source of the Nile, or that Stanley really found Dr. Livingstone. As a matter of fact, some of his explorations are financed by Belgium when the British government fails to support his ventures. It is not until Queen Victoria presents him with a gold, diamond-studded snuffbox, together with a congratulatory letter, that his accomplishments are accepted by the British public.

An extraordinary novel is *The Narrow Path, an African Childhood*, by Francis Selorney (Frederick A. Praeger). Kofi is a lonely child who lives on the coast of Ghana with his parents. His father, who is the village schoolmaster, is a stern disciplinarian and wants Kofi to walk the straight and narrow path of model behavior. Kofi is an honest boy, but he has a touch of mischievousness in his nature and frequently gets into trouble. As a younger boy, he pits his mother against his father and enjoys hearing them quarrel. He is running to his mother's protective skirts frequently, but throughout this whole novel, written in autobiographical style, Kofi longs for a more understanding relationship with his father.

The novel presents the basic conflict between Christianity and witchcraft, and it deals with the inner compulsions of a child growing up. When Kofi, after climbing to the top of his mother's tall mound of supplies, sees a night bird, he feels like the bird, high but alone, and he experiences a strong desire to be free of his constraints.

This remarkable novel shows a boy growing up in loneliness while attempting to understand his family and longing for a happy father-son relationship. His father is well-educated, ambitious, honest, and full of pride, but he is relentless in his ambitions for his son. He knows no other way to realize these ambitions except through merciless beatings, most often administered in anger and because of a lack of understanding of the growing boy.

Another tale of loneliness is a considerably different novel. This is *North to Freedom* by Anne Holm, which has been translated from the Danish by L. W. Kingsland (Harcourt, Brace & World). This is a compellingly poignant novel written for readers twelve years of age or older. David has lived in a concentration camp for twelve years when he suddenly has a chance to escape. His odyssey takes the reader from the prison camp to Salonika, to Italy, and north to Denmark. The novel traces the gradual obliteration in David's mind of distrustfulness of other human beings and the growth of trust and love instead. David has known only the grayness of oppressive buildings. When he sees a world of green and gold, he suddenly desires life, not death. He visits different churches alone, tiptoeing in to try to discover a way of faith. Finally he creates his own deity, a god of green pastures. He thanks this god for helping him to learn about happiness and how to smile.

One of the books by Joseph Krumgold, *And Now Miguel* (Thomas Y. Crowell Co.) also gives a sense of loneliness as well as a deep feeling for the cycle of the seasons with their special work and satisfactions. Miguel wishes to become a man too rapidly, and he makes many blunders in the process. He is the son of a sheepherder in the Southwest, near Santa Fe, New Mexico. Miguel feels isolated and rejected by the older men and wishes to take his place with them when they drive the herds to the top of the Sangre de Cristo mountains.

Another novel by Krumgold, *Onion John* (Thomas Y. Crowell Co.) depicts Onion John who lives alone in Hessian hills in a stone hut containing four bathtubs with no running water. Onions are his favorite food, and he is happy with his independent, lonely existence. A young man, Andy Rusch, Jr., somehow cannot agree with his father's materialistic philosophy of life, and he goes to Onion John to seek understanding.

A Krumgold novel, *Henry 3* (Atheneum Publishers) presents another side of loneliness. Two boys, Henry 3, and his close friend, Fletcher Larkin, live in the suburb of Crestview. Henry longs for the companionship of his father, and Fletch yearns for a real family. Henry 3 has a high intelligence quotient, 154, but doesn't want the other boys to know it. The two boys have some philosophical discussions about war. When grandfather Larkin dies and leaves his estate to Fletch, the latter has an ingenious plan to destroy the suburb of Crestview. He now decides that he needs a family and asks Mrs. Levering if she and her husband can become his guardians, as a business proposition. She explains to him that families are not put together like real estate, that they involve a sense of sharing and love. His unhappy loneliness is heartbreaking when he tells her that he has never had much experience talking to a mother. One of the most pathetic scenes in the book is Fletcher's attitude of resigned disappointment when he thinks Mrs. Levering will not accept his proposition to have him in the family.

Novels of Loneliness, Courage, and Unselfishness

Two novels for younger children emphasizing loneliness and courage are *The Courage of Sarah Noble* by Alice Dalgliesh (Charles Scribner's Sons) and *The Princess and the Lion* by Elizabeth Coatsworth (Pantheon Books).

The Courage of Sarah Noble is based on a true incident involving a little girl who, in 1707, goes to cook for her father who is constructing a home in New Milford. "Keep up your courage, Sarah Noble," her mother says as she leaves home, and these words ring in the ears of the little eight-year-old girl who hears the woo-a-ooh of the owl and the howl of the wolf in the wilderness. Then one day, her father leaves her alone in the forest, and Sarah learns that being afraid takes courage also.

In *The Princess and the Lion*, an Abyssinian princess disguises herself as a male groom and embarks on a dangerous journey with Asfa, her mule, and Menelik, the lion, to Mount Wachni, where her brother, Prince Michael, and other princes are imprisoned. It is her purpose to inform him that he has been selected to be the next king of Abyssinia, and to warn him not to escape lest he lose his right to rule the kingdom. Throughout the journey, the princess and her animal companions are subjected to torrential storms, crocodile-infested waters, and capture by a slave caravan.

A third novel for younger children that brings out the beauty that lies in serving others is *A Charm for Paco's Mother* by Louise A. Stinetorf (John Day Co.). Paco wants desperately to pray at the great stone cross on Christmas Eve for a miracle to restore his mother's sight. But circumstances do not make Paco's journey easy, and he finds too many others needing help before he can reach the cross on the mountain. There is the little kid which Paco must rescue from the rabbit snare. Then the wheels break down on Zorrio's cart, and his little girl, Malinchina, must be cared for while he searches for the right tree for a new wheel. There is a friend who cannot find his way to Mitla and must be entertained in the home. The little charcoal worker, Miguel, also needs protection from the cold, and so Paco gives up his own warm serape to the child shivering in his coat of flapping palm leaves.

A small novel of sensitive beauty is *Trail of Apple Blossoms* by Irene Hunt (Follett Publishing Co.). This is the tale of the Bryant family's struggles on their journey across the wilderness from Boston to the Midwest. Hoke Bryant and his sister meet Johnny Appleseed who dreams of beauty for the new land as he leaves a trail of apple blossoms along his way. But being also a practical woodsman as well as a dreamer, Johnny Appleseed wears his porridge pot on top of his head when he has too many seedlings to carry.

Another novel of beauty and sadness by Irene Hunt is *Across Five Aprils* (Follett Publishing Co.). The author uses the symbol of blooming lilacs to represent the passage of a year's time during the Civil War. The novel concerns a southern Illinois family's struggles between national patriotism and innate loyalty to southern tradition. Jethro Creighton, a boy of ten, takes on the burdens of the male adults in his family when the latter go off to war. His mother, Ellen Creighton, is both practical and sensitive. The novel is permeated with a sense of beauty made somewhat more poignant by the tragedies of war. Jethro feels "a lonely ache" at the spectacle of ghostly clouds suffused with a misty purple haze. The tune of April brings a sound of poetry to his consciousness as he gazes lovingly at the brown furrows of upturned earth shining in the sunlight.

Maia Wojciechowska has written two novels which have the theme of loneliness. In *Shadow of a Bull* (Atheneum Publishers), one senses the loneliness and fear of Manolo Olivar who wants to live his own life and not be a matador like his father, Juan Olivar, the most famous bullfighter in Spain. No one wants to let Manolo have a choice of vocation for his future. He has no *afición* or urge to fight bulls. In Spain, people like to watch heroes cheat death. Manolo kneels in front of La Macarena and begs for a miracle. He does not want to show fear to others, and it is Alfonso Castillo who reassures the boy by stating that a man's life can be many things, and one must be true to one's self.

A second novel by Maia Wojciechowska is *A Single Light* (Harper & Row, Publishers). This is the story of a girl who is deaf and dumb, the daughter of Ramón de Prada. The locale is the village of Almas in Andalucia in the southern part of Spain. Because she is a mute, the girl is ostracized by the villagers. When her mother dies, the distracted father takes the child to the home of her grandfather where she is given the duty of tending goats. She loves the clouds and the stark hills, and the sensation of the wind whistling through the trees, and she is happy with the animals. But, living in a world of unbroken silence, she longs for the closeness, the touch, of a human being. Later, when she is fifteen years old, she is asked to care for a neighbor's baby, and she is happy to have a human being to love. But when the child she is caring for dies, the girl becomes the subject of unpleasant village gossip. Rejected by a father who neither loves nor hates her, she eventually goes to the parish house to serve the priest. Then, during her third week there, when she is alone in the church, a miracle occurs. The miracle of the statue changes the lives of many people.

A rather frightening book by this same author, and one which probably should be read only by adults or by mature adolescents, is *Tuned Out* (Harper & Row, Publishers), a tale of hippies, marihuana, LSD, and disillusionment.

Another form of loneliness is the craving for old friends and the familiar way of life which are suddenly lost to one. An unforgettable story of this type, for both children and adolescents, is *The Light in the Forest* by Conrad Richter (Bantam Pathfinder Editions). The author perceptively handles the agony of a fifteen-year-old boy who is wrenched from the security of his Indian life and plunged into the society of the white man. True Son suffers deeply when Cuyloga, his Indian father, gives him back to his white father, Henry Butler, when his white mother, Myra Butler, becomes ill. The child battles like a panther to keep his freedom when the time comes for him to be returned to the white man's home. He detests his real name, John Cameron Butler, and he loathes pants, jackets, and heavy boots, symbols of white man's treachery. He feels enclosed in a bedroom and longs for his Indian father and his free Indian life in the woods where he can sleep in the out-of-doors.

A loneliness comparable to True Son's is that of Hetty Petrie in the gripping novel, *The Far-Off Land* by Rebecca Caudill (The Viking Press). Hetty leaves her life of security with the Moravians to go to the "far-off-land." She learns from Sister Oesterlein that she need not be afraid of wilderness ways if she loves all people, and that she must show reverence for God, and life, and all lovely things on the earth. The girl has many lonely moments but with the help of Tish, she maintains steadfast courage and determination to face hardships, and eventually she learns to enjoy the strange land.

Enrichment Ideas Related to Literature of Loneliness

Children can read novels relating to this theme and then select some of the following activities which might help to give a better understanding of the various forms of loneliness.

General Creative Activities

Writing Diaries: Pupils can read at least two novels which have the theme of loneliness coupled with the necessity for ingenuity and courage. They can imagine that they are permanently isolated from society. A diary can be written as if the pupil were Selkirk in the book, *The Monarch of Juan Fernandez* by Ballard, Karana in *Island of the Blue Dolphins* by O'Dell, or Ishi in *Ishi, Last of His Tribe,* by Kroeber.

Drawing a Treasure Map: Children may use any of the three books mentioned above, or books of similar content, to develop a treasure map showing the location of buried treasure. An expository paragraph can be written with a title like "How to Get to the Treasure of Johnston Island." A treasure map can also be drawn of events in *The King's Fifth* or in *Walk the World's Rim.*

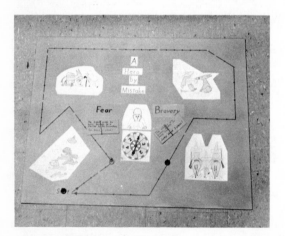

Loneliness and Fear
Game on Fear developed by Erasimo Bruno
Cal-State College,
Hayward, California

Creating an Original Game: Most characters in these books have shown instances of fear and courage. An original game of fear and courage, based on instances which really indicated fear or courage in the novel, can be created. This may be similar to the illustrated game developed by Erasimo Bruno, and based on *Hero by Mistake* by Anita Brenner (William R. Scott). A pictorial map is placed on a chip board. Accompanying cards list instances of fear or courage which are shown in *Hero by Mistake*. Pupils use a spinner and get a number. The number refers to a card. The card might say, for instance, "Dionisio feared the darkness. Go back three spaces." or "Dionisio threw stones at the wolf. Move ahead five spaces." The first player to reach an assigned goal wins the game.

Loneliness and Fear
Shadowgraph Figures by
Erasimo Bruno
for **A Hero by Mistake**
Cal-State College,
Hayward, California

Finding and Using Picturesque Speech Examples: Boys and girls can read *Ishi, Last of His Tribe* or *Island of the Blue Dolphins* and compile a list of picturesque speech or examples of appropriate and colorful similes, metaphors, personification, alliteration, or refrains. A paragraph can be written describing a lonely or a fearful experience. One appropriate type of metaphor, simile, or personification can offer more freshness to the paragraph. A recent movie, *Making Word Pictures* (Coronet) helps children to write paragraphs which are vivid and picturesque.

Writing Prayers in a Literary Style: Both *North to Freedom* by Holm, and *And Now Miguel* by Krumgold contain scenes which depict the significance of prayer. These sections can be read again and then compared or contrasted with other prayers in literature. Rumer Godden has translated *Prayers from the Ark* by Carmen Bernos de Gasztold (Viking Press). Children may wish to select an animal and create an appropriate prayer to reflect the personality of that animal, or they may wish to write prayers which would be in keeping with the circumstances facing a character. For instance, what kind of prayer might Selkirk compose? Or, what words might Tom utter when he faces death alone on that arctic tundra?

Writing Character Sketches of Krumgold's Boys: Three novels by Krumgold, *And Now Miguel, Henry 3,* and *Onion John,* depict three totally different boys, but each expresses loneliness and a lack of adult sensitivity toward the feelings of a boy with "growing pains." Pupils can write a character sketch of a boy from one of these novels and contrast it with a character from another Krumgold book. Two poems in *People I'd Like to Keep* entitled "Darling Doctor de Plunkett," and "Miss Hortense Rogers, the Grade School Principal," by Mary O'Neill (Doubleday & Co.), depict persons who understand the problems of a girl. Attitudes of adults in a Krumgold book might be contrasted with those in the O'Neill volume of poems.

Dressing Dolls in Historic Costumes: When girls have been up-rooted from their early homes, they have found solace in dolls which they carried with them from their old to their new abode. Doll clothes fashioned in the style of the times give a realistic picture of early life. Girls can design and sew doll clothes which depict historical years such as those of the Revolutionary or Civil Wars. *The Costume Book* by Joseph Leeming (J. P. Lippincott Co.) has pictures of costumes of various historical periods.

Activities Related to the Culture of the Far North

Creating Original Chants, Songs, and Dramas: One novel about arctic wastelands and the dangers inherent in their conquest can be read. Pupils can imagine that they are Akavak, Elli, or Inatuk. An original song using a chant or refrain in which dangers are recounted can be created. Two pupils may wish to create the song together. Some pupils may do role playing, creative movement, or pantomimes to reenact a scene from one of these books.

Dancing the Eskimo Dance Song: Eskimo families which existed on isolated lands depended heavily on the seal for food and imple-ments. *The Story of Comock the Eskimo* edited by Edmund Carpenter (Simon & Schuster) speaks of the importance of the seal hunt. The Pisak Eskimo dance song was composed by a Coppermine River native in the Northwest Territory. The song speaks of patient eyes watching for the seal to come up to its breathing hole. Eskimos sing in the "dance house" and compose dances spontaneously. The Pisak dance is one which is done in the center of a circle by a lone dancer who beats the drum and hops to its rhythm, first on both feet and then on alternating feet. When he finishes his song and dance, he signals for another tribesman to take his place. (*Music Far and Near,* 4, page 81, by James L. Mursell, et. al. Teachers' Edition).

Carving Soap Figures: Eskimos and other primitive tribes frequently carve from walrus tusks or from stone. Pupils can carve figures of seals, dogs, or birds from soap. The book *Soap Sculpture* by Lester Gaba, and illustrated with photographs (Franklin Watts) offers practical suggestions for soap carving and the painting of soap. A bar of white floating soap and simple tools such as a kitchen paring knife or a penknife can be used to make beautiful figures. Some carved art work by Eskimos is photographed in *The Art of the Eskimo* by Shirley Glubok, with special photography by Alfred H. Tamarin, (Harper & Row).

Creating Story Boards: Picture stories are carved on boards covering the walls of houses in Koror, one of the Micronesian Islands. Pupils can design story boards similar to the Micronesian ones by retelling in pictorial form *The Story of Comock the Eskimo* as told to Robert Flaherty and edited by Edmund Carpenter (Simon and Schuster).

Imaginative Survival Lessons Using Recordings: One exciting biographical novel is *Alone* by Richard E. Byrd (G. P. Putnam's Sons). Byrd's experiences in the white polar wastelands help readers to value the courage and resourcefulness of men fighting for survival against hostile nature. "Polar Pilot, the Richard Byrd Story," is one of the recordings of the Imagicraft Series, produced by Bert F. Cunnington and E. Paul Torrance (Ginn and Co.). The disc included in this recording package has three "integrated survival exercises." Several lessons designed to improve the art of observation appear in the *Teachers' Guide and Recorded Text* which accompanies this story as well as "Sweetheart of the Skies, the Amelia Earhart Story." Pupils will enjoy listening to the recording and doing the observation lessons.

Clay and Plaster Modeling Experiences: Many stories mentioned in this chapter tell about Eskimos, primitive cavemen, or Indians, and about their religious beliefs and their forms of worshipping various spirits. Usually, a carved replica of a nature object was worshipped or used to ward off demons.

A book by Richard Slade entitled *Modeling in Clay, Plaster and Papier-Mâché* (Lothrop, Lee & Shepard Co.) offers a section on clay modeling. Beginning with basic shapes, the author advances to cubes, spheres, and cones, and shows how one can model. The second chapter gives simple directions for making plastic tiles. A design can be transferred to the plaster tile by tracing it through thin paper. After this, it can be gouged out with a linoleum-cutting tool. These cut-out places can be decorated with colored plaster. Directions are given for figures over armatures, and for simple casting in relief. Pupils can model characters from novels they have read.

Directions for doing simple papier-mâché modeling, including work over a balloon or a wire mesh armature or figure, are given. The pulp method of modeling papier-mâché is also explained. The author suggests the use of Boneware self-hardening clay which can be obtained from Sculpture House, Inc., 38 East 30th Street, New York, New York 10016. Some art stores sell clay that can be hardened in kitchen ovens at low temperature. An example of this kind of clay is Ceraclay, which can be obtained from the F. Stewart Clay Company, 133 Mulberry Street, New York, New York 10013.

G. C. Payne has written *Adventures with Clay* which has 49 plates and 88 drawings (Frederick Warne & Co.). Pupils can read this book and then make mosaic tiles or pottery pieces depicting scenes from folktales and legends, or they can make animals about which they have read in any of the novels mentioned in this chapter.

Activities Based on "The Light in the Forest"

Illustrated Posters or Book Blurbs: In the novel, *The Light in the Forest,* Richter has many expressions of great poetic beauty. Students can create colorful posters listing some of the similes and metaphors

Papier Mache Indian Figure
True Son, character of
A Light in the Forest
Cal-State College,
Hayward, California

from the novel, or they can design book blurbs which use picturesque language to outline the plot.

Writing Character Sketches of Contrast: Pupils can write descriptive character sketches which contrast certain characters in *The Light in the Forest*. They can contrast True Son with Del Hardy, or Myra Butler with Aunt Kate, or other characters in this story with characters in other novels.

Creating Imaginary Conversations: Children can imagine that they are True Son talking to his Indian father about the Butlers. Or, they can develop an imaginary conversation in which the Butlers discuss True Son.

Activities Based on Novels by Irene Hunt

Writing Correspondence about Imaginary Situations: Across Five Aprils is a narrative of war events through the use of correspondence which deals with significant episodes. After reading the complete novel, pupils may refer back to the various letters in the book. Some recent events, such as the war in Vietnam, or disasters caused by earthquakes, hurricanes, tidal waves, or cyclones, or mining or industrial accidents, can be chosen. Two people in the class can correspond with each other about the same event. One person is directly involved in the tragedy. The other is not at the scene. Letters will be more interesting if specific incidents are included and if colorful adjectives are used.

Pretending to be Newspaper Correspondents: The style of special newspaper correspondents from local periodicals can be studied. Some events in the novel, *Across Five Aprils*, can be retold as if the pupils were correspondents.

Comparing Non-Standard Dialect with Standard Dialect: The novel, *Across Five Aprils*, includes several examples of non-standard dialect or language which indicates a lack of formal education. A class committee can discover instances where non-standard dialect is used. These language excerpts can be rewritten in formal literary or standard dialect and then compared with the honesty and feeling of the original passage.

Painting Watercolor Scenes or Writing Poetry or Descriptive Paragraphs: Several selections in *Across Five Aprils* describe the seasons in beautiful, poetic prose. For instance, pages 49-52 present autumn in its somber colors of yellow-golds and browns. These pages can be recorded on tape. After pupils listen to the recording several times, they can paint a scene with watercolors, or they can write a poem in free or blank verse, recreating the autumn scene. Page 52 includes a paragraph or two which contain aural imagery. Cries and sounds are emphasized throughout the entire paragraph. A descriptive paragraph which focuses upon aural imagery can be written. This can be the sound of the subway, various street sounds, sounds at the airport or in the skies, or sounds heard in the rural out-of-doors.

Collecting Examples of Picturesque Speech: Irene Hunt uses similes and metaphors beautifully. Her picturesque language is always appropriate and clear. Sentences and phrases which have vivid metaphoric effect can be collected from the novel, *Across Five Aprils.* For instance, on page 8, the skin of Ellen Creighton is compared to the dryness of leather; and on page 101, the silence of Dave Burdow is likened to darkness.

Writing Paragraphs of Contrast: The John Newbery Medal was awarded to Irene Hunt for *Up a Road Slowly* (Follett Publishing Co.) This unusual novel shows the gradual development of Laura from a frightened, emotionally disturbed child to a gracious adolescent of seventeen. The author has created clear, deft images of Aunt Cordelia and Uncle Haskell. Pupils can compare a character in *Up a Road Slowly* with one in *Across Five Aprils.* For instance, Aunt Cordelia can be contrasted with Ellen Creighton, or Jethro's inner feelings and sensitivity can be compared to those of Laura.

Activities Based on the Johnny Appleseed Theme

Comparing Novels about Johnny Appleseed: Johnny Appleseed has become an American legend. Numerous versions have been told of the exploits of Jonathan Chapman who was nicknamed Johnny Appleseed by his fellow pioneers. The Hunt version, *Trail of Apple Blossoms* (Follett Publishing Co.), while not a complete biography, does, with a keen sense of appreciation for religion and beauty, depict Johnny's love of nature and his affection for the Indians. Other tales about this legendary figure can be found. Some of these are *Better Known as Johnny Appleseed* by Mabel Leigh Hunt (J. B. Lippincott Co.) and *Little Brother of the Wilderness,* the Story of Johnny Appleseed, by Meridil Le Suer (Alfred A. Knopf), which is for younger children. Pupils can compare facts in any one of these versions with those in the Hunt volume.

Creating and Producing a Johnny Appleseed Operetta: A committee of gifted pupils can write or produce an operetta by expanding upon episodes in *Trail of Apple Blossoms* by Irene Hunt. As Johnny Appleseed journeyed westward, he carried his Bible and a bag of apple seeds. He hated the killing of men or animals. Children can consult music books to find appropriate songs related to the story plot, or they can try to find relevant recordings. For instance, an Alsatian folk song, "The Life that's Free," with words by Florence Hoare, speaks of the joy of streams and of wild deer. (*Music for Living, Near and Far,* Book 4, Silver Burdett Co.). Another song which could be used and which appears in this same book is "Now All the Woods Are Sleeping," a chorale by Johann Sebastian Bach, with words translated by Catherine Winkworth. Older children could use the poem on Johnny Appleseed from Vachel Lindsay's *Johnny Appleseed and Other Poems* (Macmillan Co.).

An Apple Festival Day: The trail of the apple blossom has been significant in American legend and history. A committee of pupils may wish to prepare an apple festival program for a special day. A filmstrip on the Johnny Appleseed Legend (Series No. 7820) produced by Encyclopaedia Britannica Educational Corp. (Chicago, Ill.), or the movie, "Johnny Appleseed—A Legend of Frontier Life," produced by Coronet Films (Chicago, Ill.), can be shown. A choral verse group could recite "Johnny Appleseed 1775-1847," which appears in *A Book of Americans* by Rosemary and Stephen Vincent Benét (Holt, Rinehart & Winston). A pageant or some tableaus can be enacted, using scenes from books about Johnny Appleseed, or from *Tree of Freedom* by Rebecca Caudill (Viking Press). This latter novel is about everyday living problems during the Revolutionary War Period, but much of the plot concerns Stephanie who tends the sprouts of her apple tree which she calls the "tree of freedom." Pupils can listen to Robert Frost reading "After Apple Picking," from the Caedmon recording TC 1060, or they can read his poems, "After Apple Picking" or "The Cow in Apple Time." Both poems appear in *Complete Poems of Robert Frost* (Holt, Rinehart & Winston). Of course, apple dumplings, apple pie, apple cider, or just apples can be served as refreshments. Some of the girls may want to do research in old cookbooks and then compile a book of apple recipes.

Activities Based on "The Black Pearl"

Writing Paragraphs of Description and Exposition: The Black Pearl by Scott O'Dell (Houghton Mifflin Co.) gives considerable information about the pearl fishing industry in the vicinity of La Paz. Suggested titles for a three-paragraph essay to be written by the pupils are "La Paz Pearling" or "Salazar and Son Pearling Industry." Or, a one-paragraph description entitled "Pearl of the World" may be composed.

Dioramas and Paintings of the Manta Diablo: On the basis of all the descriptions of the Manta Diablo given in *The Black Pearl,* children may write a paragraph depicting their mental image of the monster, or they may paint a picture of him. Some of the pupils may wish to construct a marine diorama showing the natives in their pearl fishing boats attacking the Manta Diablo.

Role Playing of Scenes from "The Black Pearl": A scene from *The Black Pearl* can be selected and dramatized. An exciting one might be taken from pages 59-64 when villagers discover the Pearl of the World. Another scene might be developed from pages 71-79 which tell how the pearl merchants try to purchase the Pearl of Heaven from the Salazars.

Writing an Additional Episode for a Novel: An additional episode for *The Black Pearl* can be written. For example, Ramon can have more experiences with a pearl dealer who begs for the pearl. Or, the old superstitious Indian who refused to take his share of the reward for the pearl might reenter the story.

Writing Words or Music for a Hymn: Father Gallardo's receiving the Pearl of Heaven for the Madonna is a major episode in *The Black Pearl*. Words and music for a hymn to the Madonna of the Pearl can be written. Or, appropriate words about the Pearl of Heaven may be written to accompany hymn music that has been selected by the pupils.

Making Charts Contrasting Two Novels about Pearls: Intellectually advanced upper grade children may read *The Pearl* by John Steinbeck (Viking Press). One committee may compile a large chart showing similarities between the two novels. A second committee may wish to compile a chart showing differences.

Oral Language Activities

Participating in Grouptalk: Dr. Babette Whipple has coined the term "grouptalk" to define a type of structured discussion which is conducted in small groups. There are specific rules to be followed, and these rules are directed so that all persons in the group contribute relevant statements to the discussion which is summarized at the end.

Techniques are explained by James Moffett in *A Student-Centered Language Arts Curriculum, Grades K-13*: A Handbook for Teachers (Houghton Mifflin Co.). Procedures are somewhat as follows: (1) A question is asked such as "What are some of the feelings which persons have when they are lonely?" Five or six students discuss the question under the direction of a pupil leader, as the teacher circulates throughout the room among the various groups to see that pupils function cooperatively. (2) Everyone is given an opportunity to answer the question. If a child cannot think of an idea, the leader may remind him to think back about times of loneliness which he has felt. (3) All members of the group listen intently to responses by others because each person is expected to come back to the question again; also in this case, pupils should have read some literature with the predominant theme of loneliness. (4) Responses to the question must be relevant. Group members are asked to keep to the subject. For example, in discussing lonesomeness, a child might begin to talk about *Boy Alone* by Reginald Ottley but wander from the subject and talk instead about fear or things that have frightened him, such as snakes. (5) Each member of the group is expected to summarize the principal point of the discussion.

Grouptalk is similar to most forms of group discussion, but direct attention to keeping to the point and to summarizing the main point of discussion keeps such conversational periods more controlled. The Moffett volume contributes many ideas on methods of improving discussion periods, and it presents numerous approaches to drama and writing.

Participating Orally in a Study of Novels: Another book, by Wilma M. Possien, which is directed to oral communication skills is *They All Need to Talk*: Oral Communication in the Language Arts Program (Appleton-Century-Crofts). The author provides guides to the development of many conversation skills such as buzz sessions, panels, and debates. Also suggested are many oral book reports such as imaginary interviews with authors, an author's speech to the class, or "Meet the Press" meetings. Additional ideas on stimulating broadcasting speaking skills appear in the volume *AV Instructional Media and Methods,* 3d ed. by James B. Brown, Richard B. Lewis, and Fred F. Harcleroad (McGraw-Hill Book Co.).

Creating a Television Play: Pupils may select a scene from any one of the novels mentioned in this chapter and create a television script. It is best to choose one that is exciting and full of conflict. The novels of Irene Hunt and Scott O'Dell are particularly adaptable to the creation of a television scene. The format of television script is somewhat different from that of a regular classroom drama. A book entitled *Integrated Teaching Materials,* How to Choose, Create, and Use Them, by Thomas R. Murray and Sherwin G. Swartout (David McKay Co.) offers considerable help on the production of a television script. Chapter 18 is entitled "Creating Television Programs." (Chapter 20 of this same book, entitled "Models and Puppets," gives many ideas to enliven literature selections.)

"You Were There" Program: Pupils may use a tape recorder to present a "You Were There" type of program. A master of ceremonies

or an inquiring reporter could interview Esteban Sandoval in *The King's Fifth,* or Jethro in *Across Five Aprils.* Questions of opinion about contemporary events of the period should be asked.

Panel Discussion: A committee of children can have a radio panel discussion as to whether or not Manolo, in the novel, *Shadow of a Bull,* was a coward. Arguments can be presented showing Manolo's fear and his bravery.

SELECTED REFERENCES FOR CHILDREN

BAKER, BETTY. *Walk the World's Rim.* New York: Harper & Row, 1965.

BALLARD, MARTIN. *The Monarch of Juan Fernandez.* Illustrated by A. R. Whitson. New York: Charles Scribner's Sons, 1967.

BENET, ROSEMARY and STEPHEN VINCENT. *The Book of Americans.* Illustrated by Charles Child. New York: Holt, Rinehart, & Winston, 1933.

BRENNER, ANITA. *Hero by Mistake.* New York: William R. Scott, 1953.

BYRD, RICHARD E. *Alone.* New York: G. P. Putnam's Sons, 1938.

CARPENTER, EDMUND, ed. *The Story of Comock, the Eskimo* as told to Robert Flaherty. New York: Simon and Schuster, 1968.

CAUDILL, REBECCA. *Tree of Freedom.* Illustrated by Dorothy Bayley Morse. New York: Viking Press, 1949.

––––––. *The Far-Off Land.* New York: Viking Press, 1964.

COATSWORTH, ELIZABETH. *The Princess and the Lion.* Illustrated by Evaline Ness. New York: Pantheon Books, 1965.

CUNNINGTON, BERT F., and TORRANCE, PAUL E. *Teachers' Guide and Recorded Text,* Side One, Sweetheart of the Skies: The Amelia Earhart Story; Side Two, Polar Pilot, the Richard Byrd Story. Boston: Ginn and Co., 1965.

D'AMELIO, DAN. *Taller than Bandai Mountain,* the Story of Hideyo Noguchi. Illustrated by Fred Banbery. New York: Viking Press, 1968.

DAVIS, VERNE T. *Orphan of the Tundra.* Illustrated by Judith Ann Lawrence. New York: Weybright & Talley, 1968.

DEFOE, DANIEL. *Robinson Crusoe.* Illustrated by N. C. Wyeth. New York: Charles Scribner's Sons, 1920.

DEGASZTOLD, CARMEN BERNOS. *Prayers from the Ark.* Translated by Rumer Godden. Illustrated by Jean Primrose. New York: Viking Press, 1962.

––––––. *The Creature's Choir.* Translated by Rumer Godden. Illustrated by Jean Primrose. New York: Viking Press, 1965.

FOX, PAULA. *The Stone Faced Boy.* Illustrated by Donald A. MacKay. Englewood Cliffs, N. J.: Bradbury Press, 1968.

FROST, ROBERT. *Complete Poems of Robert Frost.* New York: Holt, Rinehart & Winston, 1962 printing.

GABA, LESTER. *Soap Sculpture.* Illustrated with photographs. New York: Franklin Watts, 1969.

GEORGE, JEAN. *My Side of the Mountain.* New York: E. P. Dutton & Co., 1959.

GLUBOK, SHIRLEY. *The Art of the Eskimo.* Designed by Oscar Krauss, with special photographs by Alfred H. Tamarin. New York: Harper & Row, 1964.

HEMINGWAY, ERNEST. *The Old Man and the Sea.* New York: Charles Scribner's Sons, 1952.

HOLM, ANNE. *North to Freedom.* Translated by L. W. Kingsland. New York: Harcourt, Brace & World, 1963.

HOLMAN, FELICE. *A Year to Grow.* Illustrated by Emily Arnold McCully. New York: W. W. Norton & Co., 1968.

HOUSTON, JAMES A. *Akavak: an Eskimo Journey.* New York: Harcourt, Brace & World, 1968.

———. *Tiktá liktak: an Eskimo Legend.* New York: Harcourt, Brace & World, 1965.

———. *The White Archer: an Eskimo Legend.* New York: Harcourt, Brace & World, 1967.

HUNT, IRENE. *Trail of Apple Blossoms.* Illustrated by Don Bolognese. Chicago: Follett Publishing Co., 1968.

———. *Across Five Aprils.* Chicago: Follett Publishing Co., 1964.

———. *Up a Road Slowly.* Chicago: Follett Publishing Co., 1966.

HUNT, MABEL LEIGH. *Better Known as Johnny Appleseed.* Decorations by James Daughtery. Philadelphia: J. B. Lippincott Co., 1950.

JOHNSON, DORIS. *Su An.* Illustrated by Leonard Weisgard. Chicago: Follett Publishing Co., 1968.

KROEBER, THEODORA. *Ishi in Two Worlds,* a biography of the last wild Indian in North America. Berkeley: University of California Press, 1963.

———. *Ishi, Last of His Tribe.* Drawings by Ruth Robbins. Berkeley: Parnassus Press, 1964.

KRUMGOLD, JOSEPH. *And Now Miguel.* Illustrated by Jean Charlot. New York: Thomas Y. Crowell Co., 1953.

———. *Onion John.* Illustrated by Symeon Shimin. New York: Thomas Y. Crowell Co., 1959.

———. *Henry 3.* Drawings by Alvin Smith. New York: Atheneum Publishers, 1967.

LAWSON, MARION. *Proud Warrior, the Story of Black Hawk.* Illustrated by W. T. Mars. New York: Hawthorn Books, 1968.

LEEMING, JOSEPH. *The Costume Book for Parties and Plays.* Drawings by Hilda Richman. Philadelphia: J. B. Lippincott Co., 1938.

LeSUEUR, MERIDIL. *Little Brother of the Wilderness,* the Story of Johnny Appleseed. Illustrated by Betty Alden. New York: Alfred A. Knopf, 1947.

LEWIS, CLAUDIA. *Poems of Earth and Space.* Illustrated by Symeon Shimin. New York: E. P. Dutton & Co., 1967.

LINDSAY, VACHEL. *Johnny Appleseed and Other Poems.* Illustrated by George Richards. New York: Macmillan Co., 23rd printing, 1967.

LUKAS, J. W., Foreword by. *The Way It Is.* Fifteen boys describe life in their neglected urban neighborhood. New York: Harcourt, Brace & World, 1969.

MONTGOMERY, JEAN. *The Wrath of Coyote.* Illustrated by Anna Siberell. New York: William Morrow & Co., 1968.

MOREY, WALT. *Kavik, the Wolf Dog.* Illustrated by Peter Parnell. New York: E. P. Dutton & Co., 1968.

MORROW, SUZANNE STARK. *Inatuk's Friend.* Boston: Little, Brown & Co., 1968.

O'DELL, SCOTT. *Island of the Blue Dolphins.* Boston: Houghton Mifflin Co., 1960.

———. *The King's Fifth.* Decorations and maps by Samuel Bryant. Boston: Houghton Mifflin Co., 1966.

——. *The Black Pearl.* Illustrated by Milton Johnson. Boston: Houghton Mifflin Co., 1967.

——. *The Dark Canoe.* Illustrated by Milton Johnson. Boston: Houghton Mifflin Co., 1968.

OTTLEY, REGINALD. *Boy Alone.* Illustrated by Clyde Pearson. New York: Harcourt, Brace & World, 1965.

RICHTER, CONRAD. *The Light in the Forest.* New York: Bantam Pathfinder Editions, 1963.

RUTHIN, MARGARET. *Elli of the Northland.* New York: Farrar, Straus & Giroux, 1968.

SELORNEY, FRANCIS. *The Narrow Path.* An African Childhood. New York: Frederick A. Praeger, 1966, 1968.

SMITH, FREDRIKA SHUMWAY. *Stanley, African Explorer.* Illustrated by Charles Moser. Chicago: Rand McNally & Co., 1968.

STEINBECK, JOHN. *The Red Pony.* Illustrated by Wesley Dennis. New York: Viking Press, Campus Book Edition, 1965.

——. *The Pearl.* New York: Viking Press, 1947.

STINETORF, LOUISA A. *A Charm for Paco's Mother.* Illustrated by Joseph Escourido. New York: John Day Co., 1965.

WEINER, SANDRA. *It's Wings that Make Birds Fly, the Story of a Boy.* New York: Pantheon Books, 1968.

WIBBERLEY, LEONARD. *Attar of the Ice Valley.* New York: An Ariel Book. Farrar, Straus & Giroux, 1968.

WOJCIECHOWSKA, MAIA. *Shadow of a Bull.* Drawings by Alvin Smith. New York: Atheneum Publishers, 1965.

——. *A Single Light.* New York: Harper & Row, 1968.

——. *Tuned Out.* New York: Harper & Row, 1968.

SELECTED REFERENCES FOR PROFESSIONALS AND ADULTS

BROWN, JAMES B; LEWIS, RICHARD B; and HARCLEROAD, FRED F. *AV Instructional Media and Methods.* 3d ed. New York: McGraw-Hill Book Co., 1968.

CARLTON, LESSIE, and MOORE, ROBERT H. *Reading, Self-Directive Dramatization and Self-Concept.* Columbus, Ohio: Charles E. Merrill Books, Bell & Howell Co., 1968.

CARTER, JAMES. *Creative Play with Fabrics and Threads.* New York: Taplinger Publishing Co., 1968.

FENWICK, SARA INNIS. *A Critical Approach to Children's Literature,* the thirty-first annual conference of Graduate Library School, August 1-3, 1966, Chicago: University of Chicago Press, 1961.

HAVILAND, VIRGINIA. *Children's Literature, a Guide to Reference Sources.* Washington, D. C.: Library of Congress, 1966.

HOLLOWELL, LILLIAN, selected and edited by. *A Book of Children's Literature,* 3d ed. New York: Holt, Rinehart & Winston, 1966.

KUNITZ, STANLEY J., and HAYCRAFT, HOWARD, eds. *The Junior Book of Authors.* Illustrated with 232 photographs and drawings. New York: H. W. Wilson Co., 1951.

MILLER, IRENE PRESTON, and LUBELL, WINIFRED. *The Stitchery Book.* Embroidery for Beginners. Drawings by Winifred Lubell. Garden City, N. Y.: Doubleday & Co., 1965.

MOFFETT, JAMES. *A Student-Centered Language Arts Curriculum, Grades K-13*: A Handbook for Teachers. Boston: Houghton Mifflin Co., 1968.

MURRAY, THOMAS R., and SWARTOUT, SHERWIN G. *Integrated Teaching Materials*, How to Choose, Create and Use Them. rev. ed. New York: David McKay Co., 1964.

MURSELL, JAMES L.; TIPTON, GLADYS; LANDECK, BEATRICE; NORDHOLM, HARRIET; FREEBURG, ROY E.; and WATSON, JACK N. *Music for Living, Near and Far*, Teachers' Book 4. Morristown, N. J.: Silver Burdett Co., 1956.

Nebraska Curriculum Development Center.
A Curriculum for English, Language Explorations for the Elementary Grades. Lincoln, Neb.: University of Nebraska Press, 1966.

Nebraska Curriculum Development Center.
A Curriculum for English, Poetry for the Elementary Grades. Lincoln, Neb.: University of Nebraska Press, 1966.

Nebraska Curriculum Development Center.
A Curriculum for English, Grade 1 Units 1-12;
A Curriculum for English, Grade 2 Units 13-22;
A Curriculum for English, Grade 3 Units 23-33;
A Curriculum for English, Grade 4 Units 34-44;
A Curriculum for English, Grade 5 Units 45-57;
A Curriculum for English, Grade 6 Units 58-70.
Lincoln, Neb.: University of Nebraska Press, 1966.

O'NEILL, MARY. *People I'd Like to Keep*. Illustrated by Paul Galdone. Garden City, N. Y.: Doubleday & Co., 1964.

PAYNE, G. C. *Adventure with Clay*. 49 plates, 88 drawings. New York: Frederick Warne & Co., 1969.

PERKINS, RALPH. *Book Selection Media*, A Descriptive Guide to 175 Aids for Selecting Library Materials. Champaign, Ill.: National Council of Teachers of English, 1966.

POSSIEN, WILMA M. *They All Need to Talk*. Oral Communication in the Language Arts Program. New York: Appleton-Century-Crofts, 1969.

RIGGS, CORINNE. *Bibliotherapy*. Newark, Del.: International Reading Association, 1968.

ROSENBERG, LILIANN KILLEN. *Children Make Murals and Sculpture*. Experiences in Community Art Projects. Photographs by Ken Wittenberg. Reinhold Publishing Corp., a subsidiary of Chapman-Reinhold, 1968.

SEIDELMAN, JAMES E., and MINTOYNE, GRACE. *Creating with Wood*. Illustrated by Lynn Sweat. London: Collier-Macmillan, Ltd., 1969.

SLADE, RICHARD. *Modeling in Clay, Plaster and Papier-Mâché*. New York: Lothrop, Lee & Shepard, 1968.

—————. *You Can Make a String Puppet*. A Practical Guide to Puppetry. Photographs by John Watts. Boston: Plays, Inc., American ed., 1966.

SMITH, JAMES STEEL. *A Critical Approach to Children's Literature*. New York: McGraw-Hill Book Co., 1967.

TOOZE, RUTH, and KRONE, BEATRICE PERHAM, eds. *Literature and Music as Resources for Social Studies*. Englewood Cliffs, N. J.: Prentice-Hall, 1955.

WILSON, H. W. *The Children's Catalog*. (Current volume and supplements.) New York: 950 University Ave., 10452.

the creative perception
of literature

For centuries, critics have used the metaphor of the mirror and the lamp to depict an aesthetic image of the literary artist. Some of their speculative philosophies appear in *The Mirror and the Lamp:* Romantic Theory and Critical Tradition, by M. H. Abrams, (New York: W. W. Norton & Co., 1958).

Enrichment Ideas does not depict the child's mind as a mirror absorbing and reflecting images from nature in an inert, quiescent manner; nor is it a lamp with focused beams flaring out from a central source. Rather, the creatively perceptive child interacts between his sensory impressions and a responsive environment with personal, emotional feeling tones so that he can explore the pages of literature joyfully with his heart, hand, and head. Literature becomes a vital life force of his personal self.

appendix:
extending learning

The following activities are designed for students who are taking college courses in children's literature or courses in the teaching of English. Students can extend their learning through individual term projects or committee reports.

Chapter 1. From Birds to Stones, The Miracle of Language

1. Study the volume *The 26 Letters* by Oscar Ogg (Thomas Y. Crowell Co.) and select one chapter for further research. For instance, the work of Patricius or Saint Patrick is little known by elementary school children. He and his followers developed "uncial" writing characters in the land of the Druids. Alcuin of York popularized the Caroline alphabet which forms the basis of many manuscript letters used today. Another style of writing is the Gothic or "black letter" script which developed in northern Europe.
2. Write a parody of portions of the *Canterbury Tales*. Use the structure of stories within a story.
3. Collect ten or fifteen alphabet books and make a comparison of the quality and style of various volumes.
4. Read some chapters from *The Miracle of Language* by Charlton Laird (Cleveland: World Publishing Co., 1953), or the paperback version of the same book printed in 1965 by Fawcett, a World Library Premier Book. Select a chapter such as "More Leaky Grammars," or "The Naughty Preposition," and create some grammar lessons for use with children. Or, consult *Winning Words* by Henry I. Christ (Boston: D. C. Heath & Co., 2d ed., 1963). Select a chapter such as "*E Pluribus Unum*" featuring foreign words and phrases, or the chapter, "The Magic of Words," and develop at least ten interesting activities for use with pupils.

5. Consult several books which tell the story of language and which have been written for adults. Rewrite some of the content in a little booklet for children titled "Adventures of Language." A few sources include:

ALEXANDER, HENRY. *The Story of Our Language.* Garden City, N. Y.: Dolphin Books, Doubleday & Co., 1962.

GIRSDANSKY, MICHAEL. *The Adventure of Language.* Englewood Cliffs, N. J.: Prentice-Hall, 1963.

SHEARD, J. A. *The Words of English.* New York: W. W. Norton & Co., 1966.

SPARKE, WILLIAM. *Story of the English Language.* Illustrated by Wayne Gallup and with photographs. New York: Abelard-Schuman, 1965.

Chapter 2.   The Wonderland of Words

1. Work on a committee to develop a thirty-minute television show on Lewis Carroll for closed circuit television. One college group made costumes, created scenery using a looking-glass and rose trees, and obtained realia including a live rabbit.
2. Listen to various recordings of *Alice in Wonderland.* Prepare listening exercises which can be used with pupils individually through the use of a classroom listening post.
3. Write a brief biography about Edward Lear for use with children. One adult biography is *Edward Lear: The Life of a Wanderer* by Vivian Noakes (Houghton Mifflin Co.).
4. Study the limerick pattern which was popularized by Lear. Collect several limericks which can be used as models by pupils who wish to create original limericks.
5. Create a parody of *The Wonderful O* by Thurber (Simon and Schuter).

Chapter 3.   Dragonflies and Frogs

1. Design an Oriental center of interest which features some form of Oriental poetry as one part of the display.
2. Work with a committee to present a thirty-minute television program on Oriental poetry.
3. Make a list of seven characteristics of *haiku* poetry and find some sample *haiku* poems to illustrate each characteristic.
4. Make a collection of photographs of objects in nature such as a sparrow, a frog, a duck, or a snake. Find some Oriental poems to accompany each photograph, or create and illustrate some original Oriental poetry.
5. Design a shadowgraph theater and shadowgraph figures. Get recordings of Oriental music and create a shadowgraph play in which some Oriental poems are depicted.

Chapter 4. The Many Faces of Aloneness

1. Write a paper on the thematic approach to literature and develop a thematic unit for use with children in the intermediate grades. Suggested themes are courage, compassion, family feelings, or understanding others. Use poems, stories, and a basic novel, or excerpts from a novel, in the development of the unit.

2. Read several books which deal with a similar theme, such as *Island of the Blue Dolphins* by Scott O'Dell, *The Monarch of Juan Fernandez* by Martin Ballard, and *Treasure Island* by Robert L. Stevenson. Develop questions and activities which might be used with children to emphasize themes such as aloneness, or ingenuity and the battle for survival.

3. Read several adventure stories listed in Chapter 4, stories which focus upon the Northland and man's conquest of arctic hardships, or stories about the primitive caveman. Write a paper on the subject, "Resourcefulness as a Quality of Man's Character." Use excerpts from books about Eskimos or Neanderthal men to develop your thesis statements concerning resourcefulness and ingenuity.

4. Select ten novels which might help pupils build positive self-concepts of themselves. One such novel is *Taller than Bandai Mountain,* the story of Hideyo Noguchi, by Dan D'Amelio (The Viking Press).

5. Read several references which offer a critical analysis of children's literature. These include: *A Critical Approach to Children's Literature* by James Steel Smith (New York: McGraw-Hill Book Co., 1967); several selections from *Readings about Children's Literature,* edited by Evelyn Rose Robinson (New York: David McKay Co., 1966); and *A Critical Approach to Children's Literature,* the thirty-first annual conference of the Graduate Library School, August 1-3, 1966, edited by Sara Innis Fenwick (Chicago: University of Chicago Press, 1967). Develop criteria for determining good children's literature and select ten novels or biographies from this chapter, or from a juvenile collection, which meet these criteria.

6. Review the publication, *Reading, Self-Directive Dramatization and Self-Concept* by Lessie Carlton and Robert H. Moore (Columbus Ohio: Charles E. Merrill Books, 1968). Select for dramatization stories which might be used to raise the self-concept of children.

7. Write a paper on compassion as reflected in children's literature.

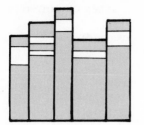

index of activities